The Big Novel

TAP!
TAP!

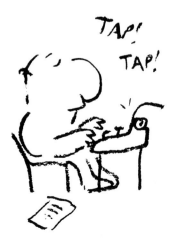

By the same author

Bed-Sit (*Jonathan Cape*)
Boxes (*Jonathan Cape*)
Calman & Women (*Jonathan Cape*)
My God (*Souvenir Press*)
The Penguin Calman
The New Penguin Calman
This Pestered Isle (*Times Newspapers Ltd*)
Couples (*The Workshop*)
Dr Calman's Dictionary of Psychoanalysis (*W. H. Allen*)
But it's my turn to leave you . . . (*Methuen*)
How about a little quarrel before bed ? (*Methuen*)
Help ! (*Methuen*)
Calman Revisited (*Methuen*)

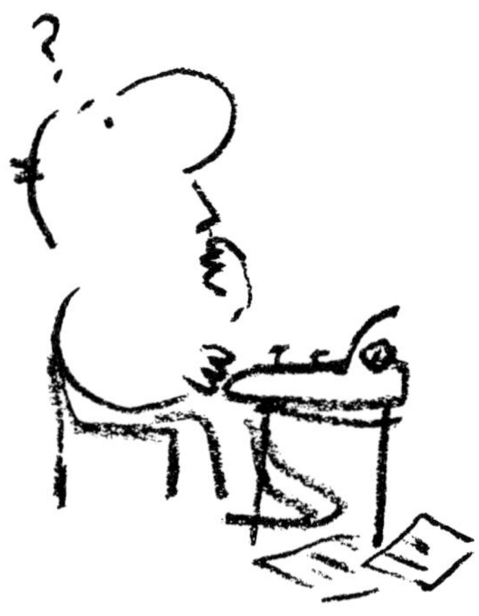

The Big Novel

By Mel Calman

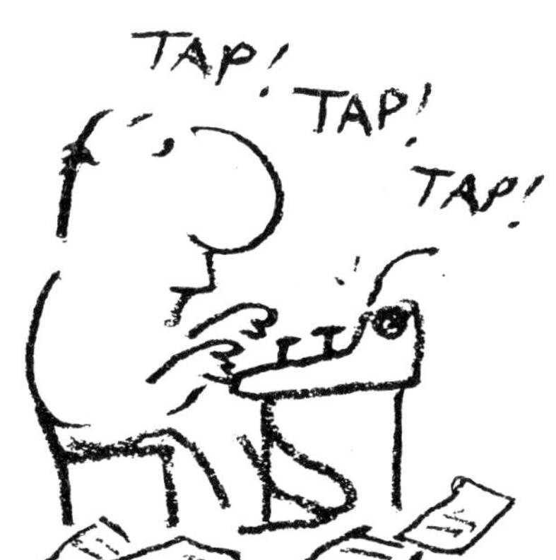
TAP! TAP! TAP!

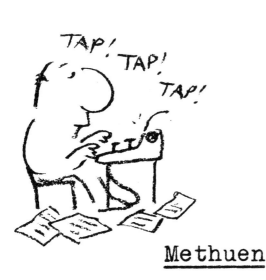

Methuen

First published 1983 by
Methuen London Ltd
11 New Fetter Lane, London EC4P 4EE

Copyright © Mel Calman 1983
Designed by Philip Thompson

ISBN 0 413 52660 7

Printed in Great Britain by
Richard Clay (The Chaucer Press) Ltd, Bungay, Suffolk

To Philip – in spite of working together . . .

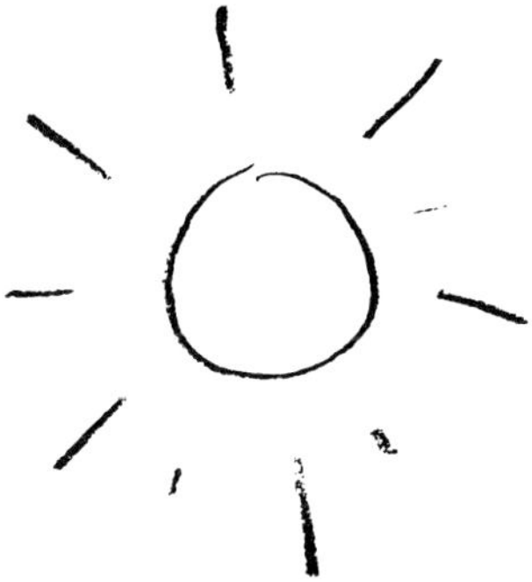

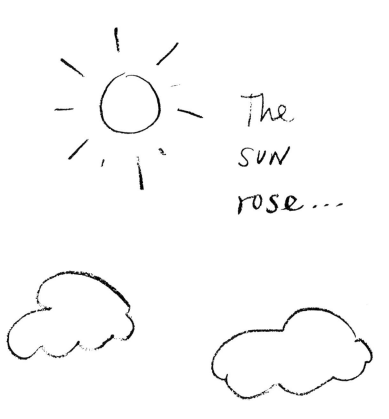

The sun rose...

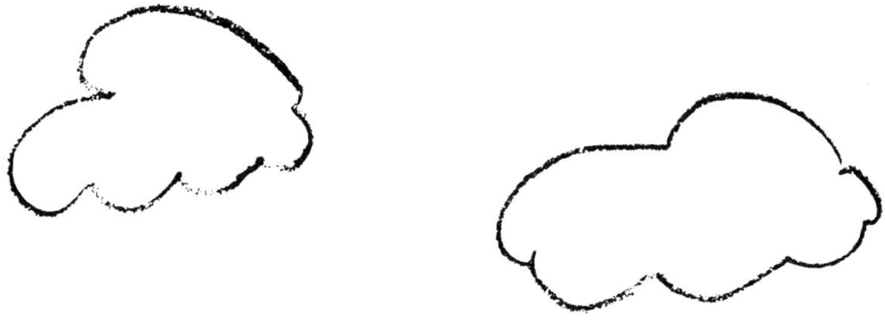

but he didn't...

INSTEAD –

He turned over
and thought about THE BIG NOVEL...

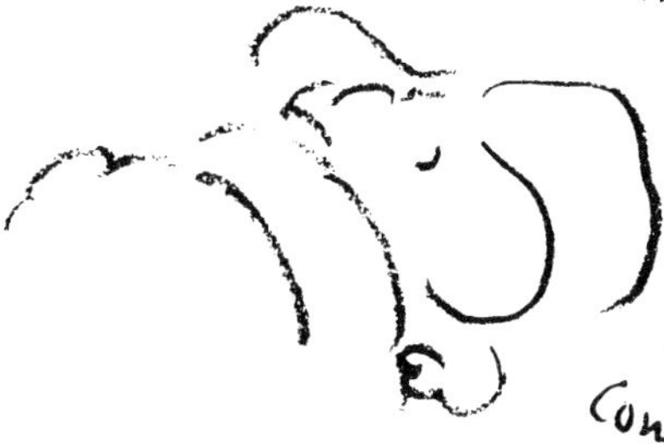

it will be wonderful..
RICH..MOVING..
poetic..
insightful..
IRONIC..
compassionate..
tender.. even
funny.. sexy..
the best..
BOOKER PRIZE..
FAME! GLORY!
WOMEN! Money!
and WOMEN!

But first a little rest -

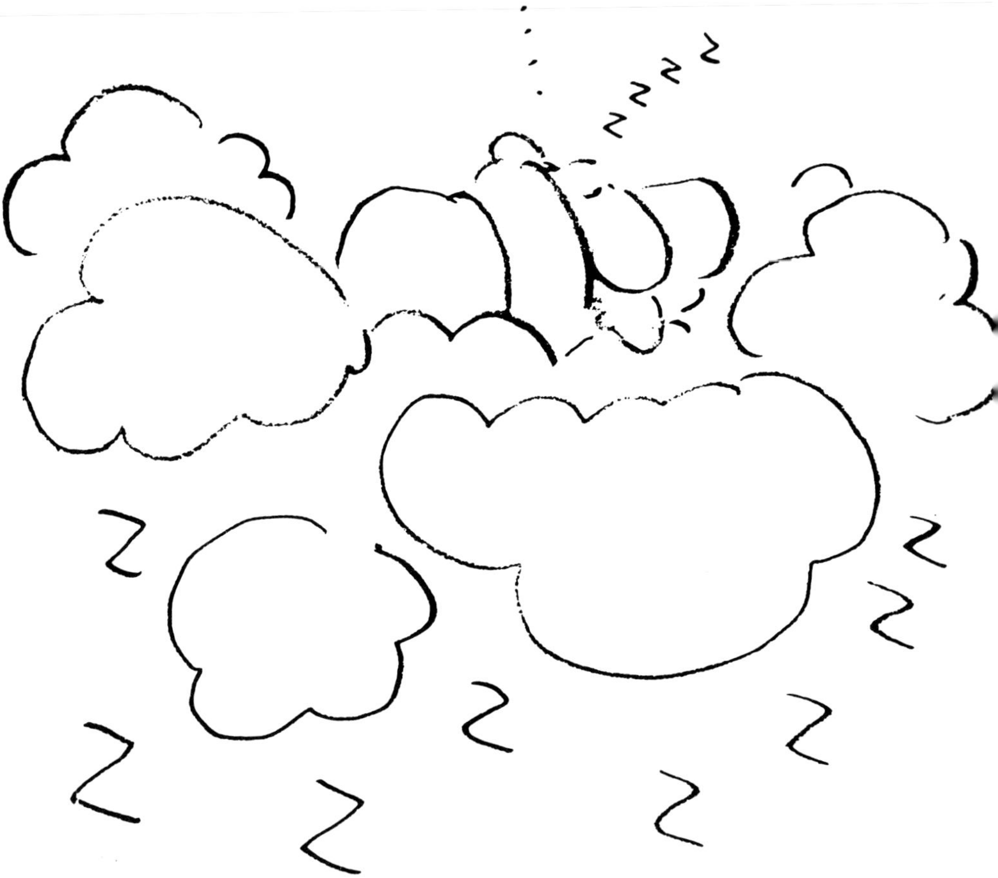

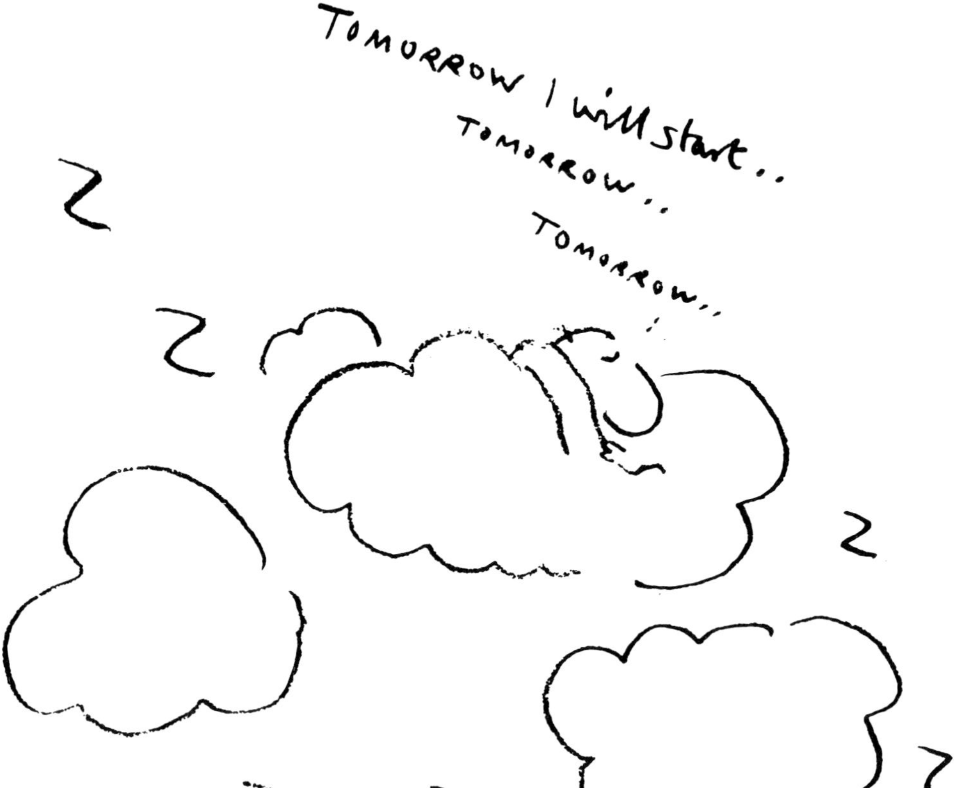
TOMORROW I will start..
TOMORROW..
TOMORROW...
Z
Z
Z
Z
Z
Z

TOMORROW comes...

as TOMORROWS tend to do...

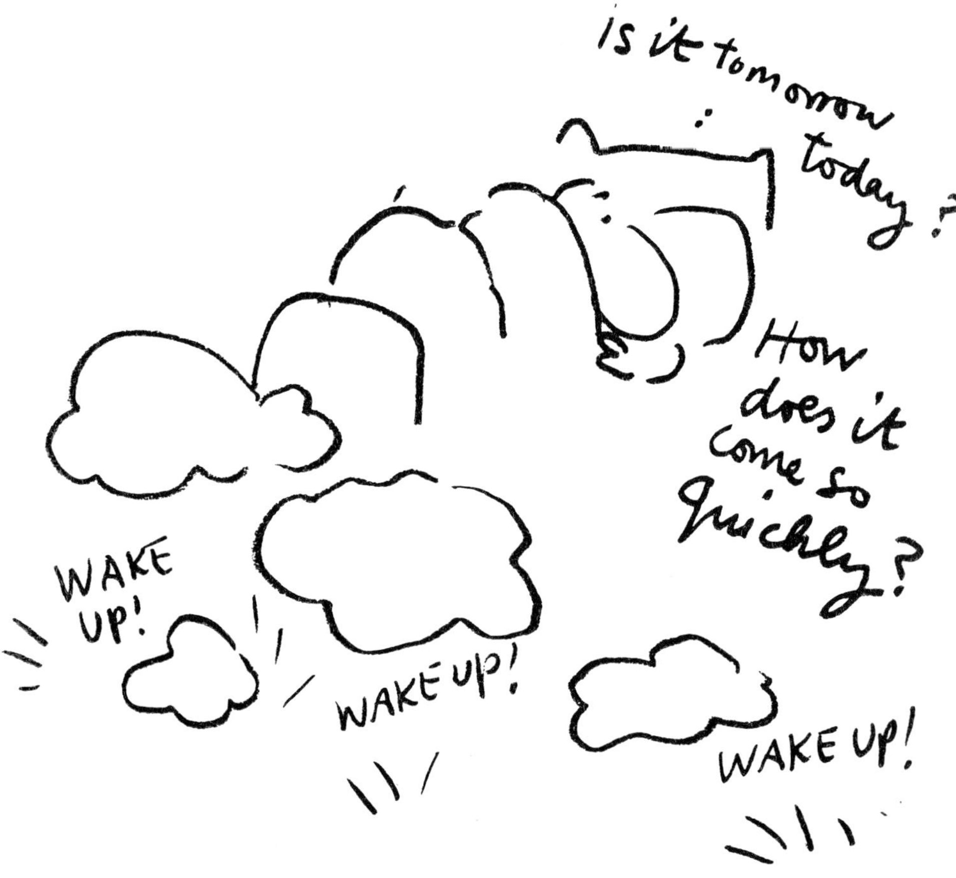
is it tomorrow today?
How does it come so quickly?
WAKE UP!
WAKE UP!
WAKE UP!

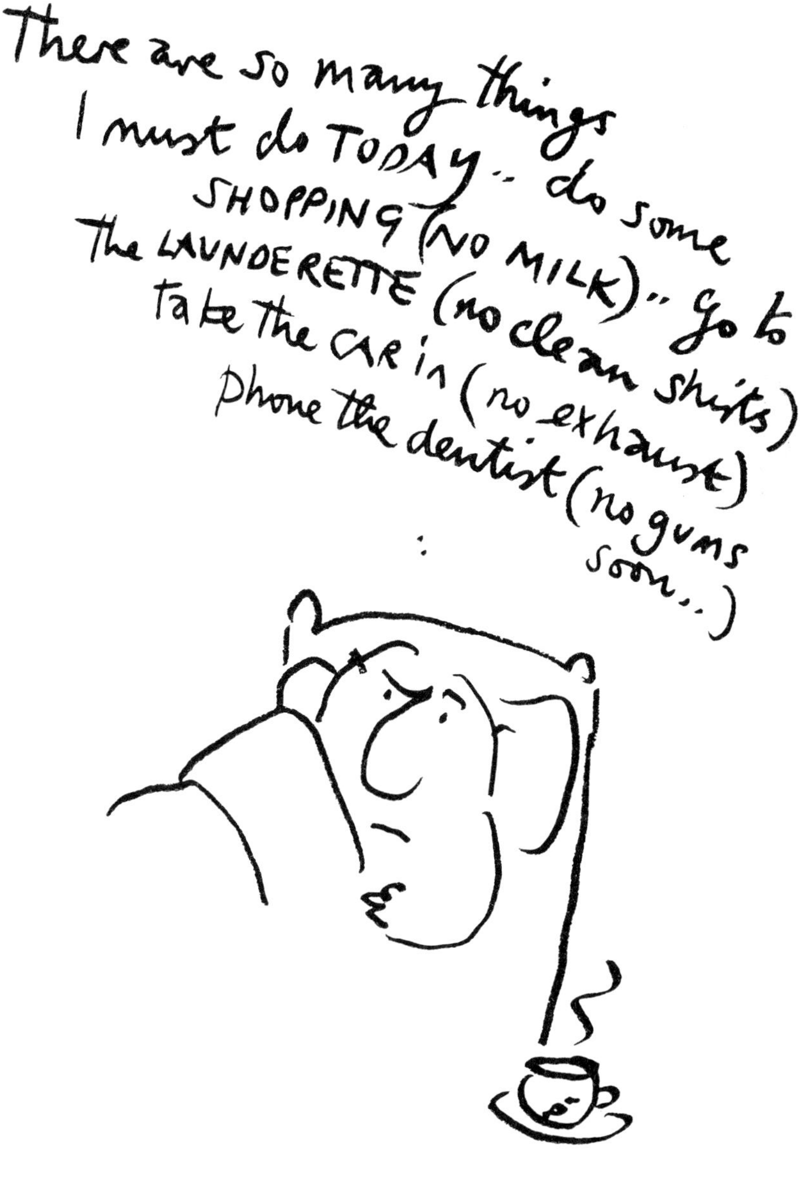
There are so many things
I must do TODAY.. do some
SHOPPING (NO MILK).. go to
The LAUNDERETTE (no clean shirts)
take the CAR in (no exhaust)
Phone the dentist (no gums
soon..)

I bet JANE AUSTEN
never had to go the
LAUNDERETTE - or TOLSTOY
to the GARAGE to have
his car fixed..
:

I suppose I could go through my old DIARIES and notebooks and search for a PLOT..

There was Helen.. she was a NOVEL in herself..

..

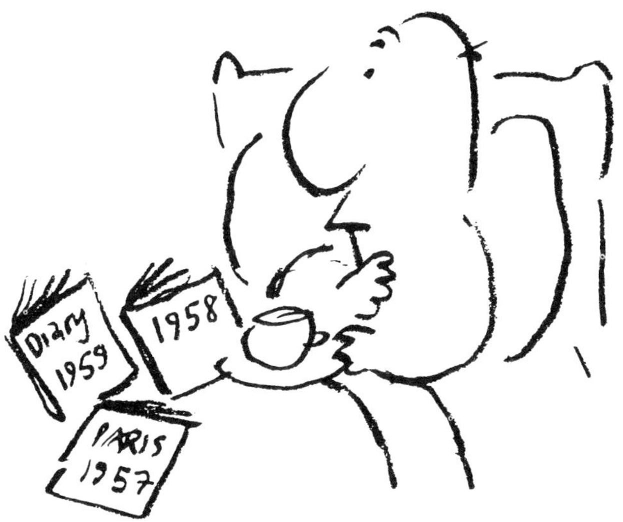
Diary 1959
1958
PARIS 1957

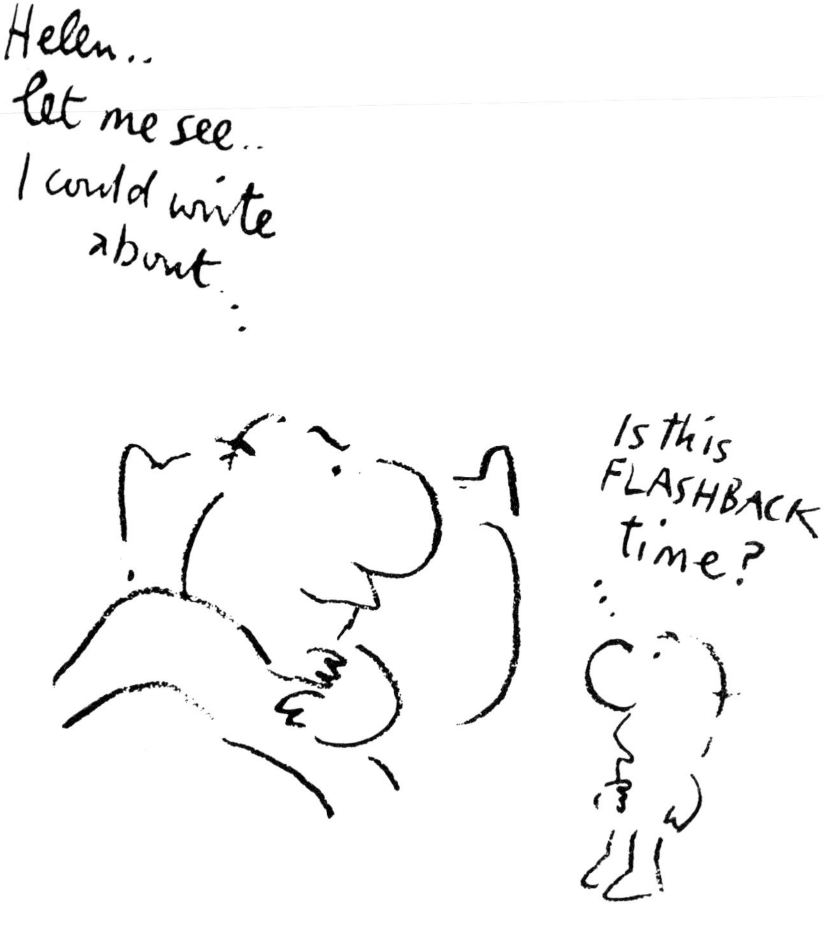
Helen..
let me see..
I could write
about...
Is this
FLASHBACK
time?

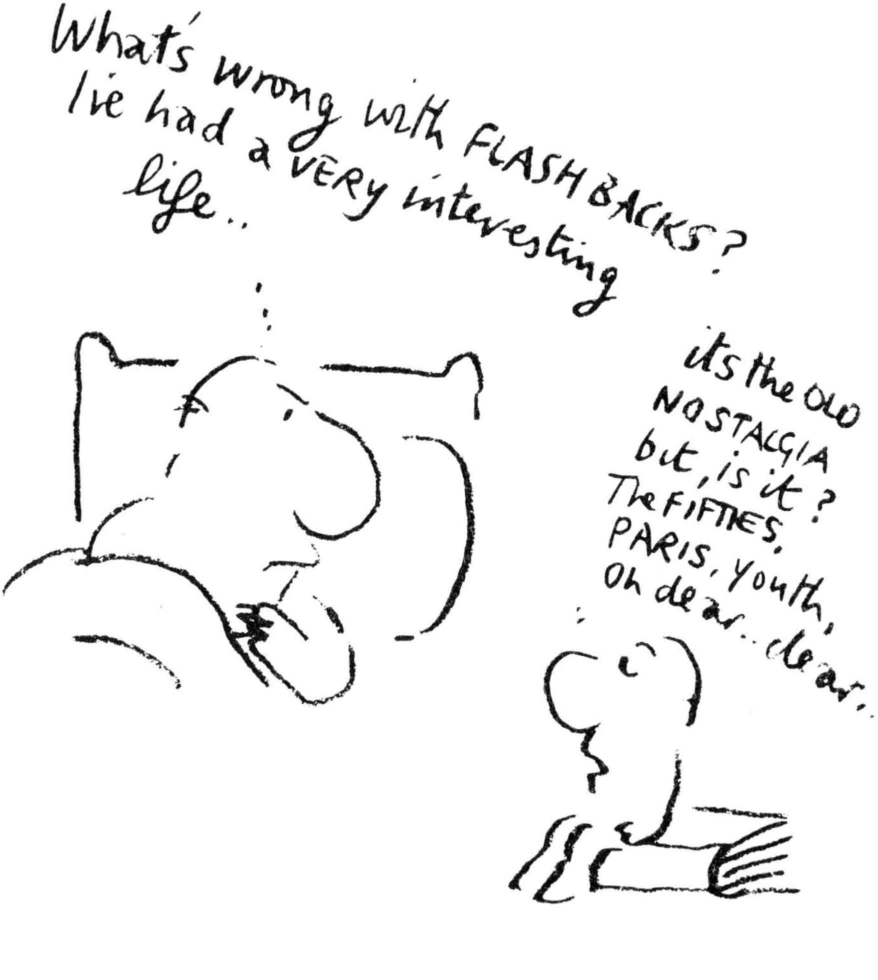
What's wrong with FLASHBACKS? I've had a VERY interesting life..
it's the OLD NOSTALGIA bit, is it? The FIFTIES. PARIS, youth, Oh dear.. dear..

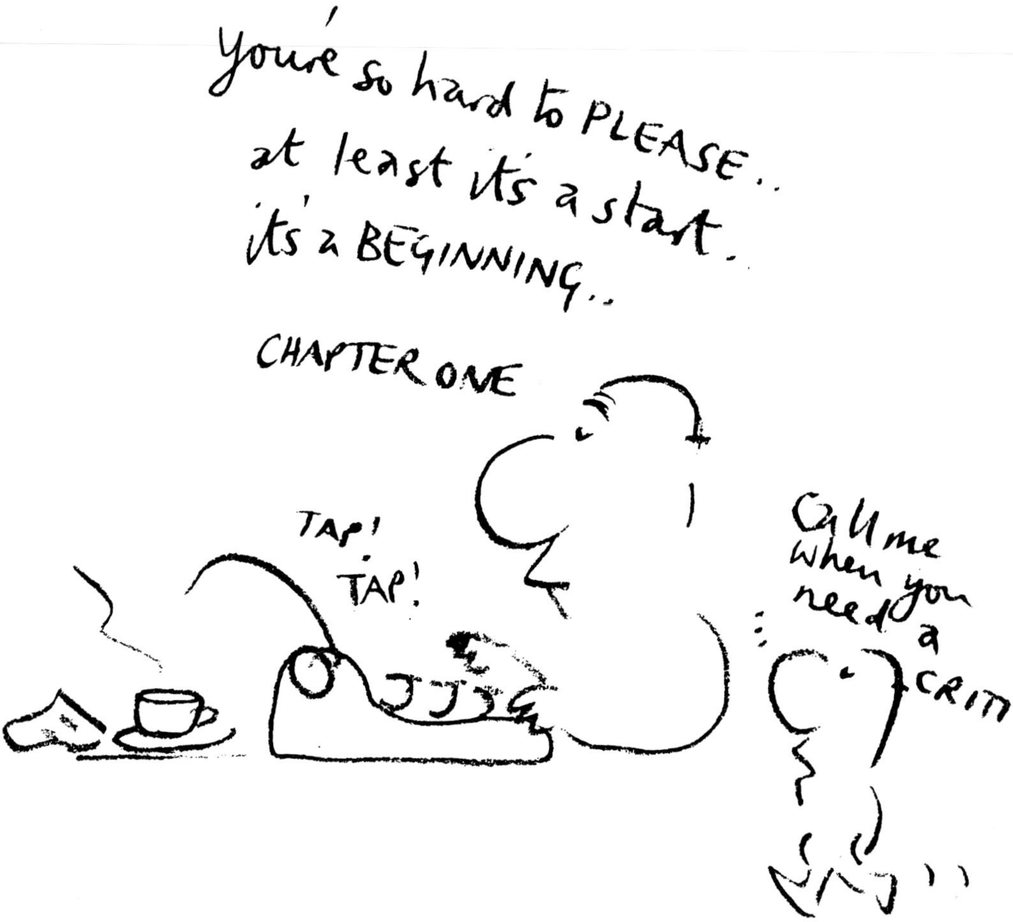
You're so hard to PLEASE..
at least it's a start.
it's a BEGINNING..
CHAPTER ONE
TAP!
TAP!
Call me when you need a CRITI

All that summer he yearned for someone to love..

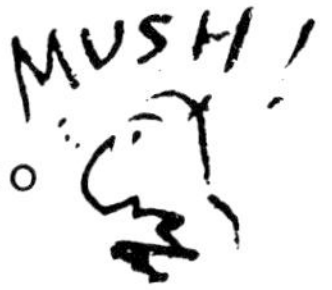
MUSH!

It was one of those parties where people kept saying 'hello' and then moving on before he could say 'hello' back. This was the permissive sixties, he thought, and still no-one had given him permission to be permissive. The only joy that night had been a long-jawed girl who worked as a resaercher for the BBC. She had pressed against him when he was trying to spoon some of the fruit punch into his glass without covering himself with pieces of orange peel. Philip knew her from some other party but before he could recollect her name she had moved on and was now thrusting her long jaw up against an account executive from Collett, Dickenson and ~~Perace.~~ Pearce. The account executive was married to an Earth Mother who lectured in anthropology and taught the Alexander Technique in her spare time. He hated parties, but still went to them in his mad desire to meet female flesh.

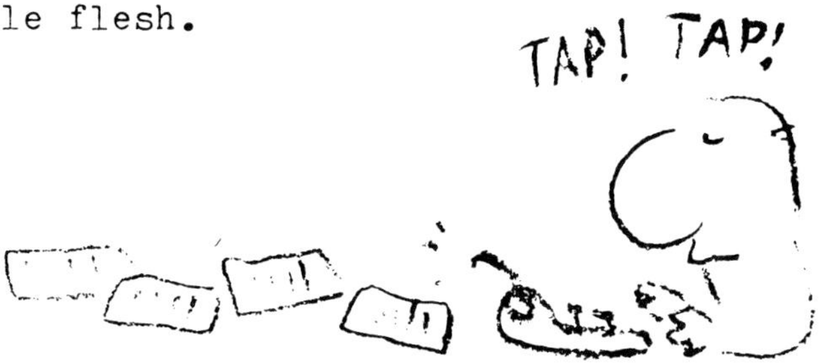
TAP! TAP!

It was a mistake. He would have just one more glass of the fruit poison and go home. A Beatles record was playing somewhere down in the basement and Philip considered moving towards the thudding sound. The host worked for The Sunday Times and had written a long profile on the Beatles.

In the far corner of the open-plan kitchen/ diner Philip could see a promising novelist (his novel about a Northern footballer who had his balls transplanted from a young bullock had attracted considerable critical acclaim) manoeuvering his hands down the front of an actress who had once done the voice-over for a Heinz commercial.

Philip felt slightly sick. He tried to rmemeber where the loo was. The thought of the avocado coloured basin made him feel even sicker..

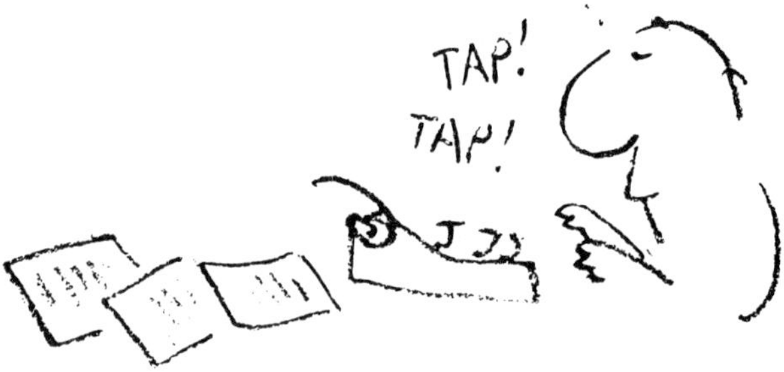
TAP!
TAP!

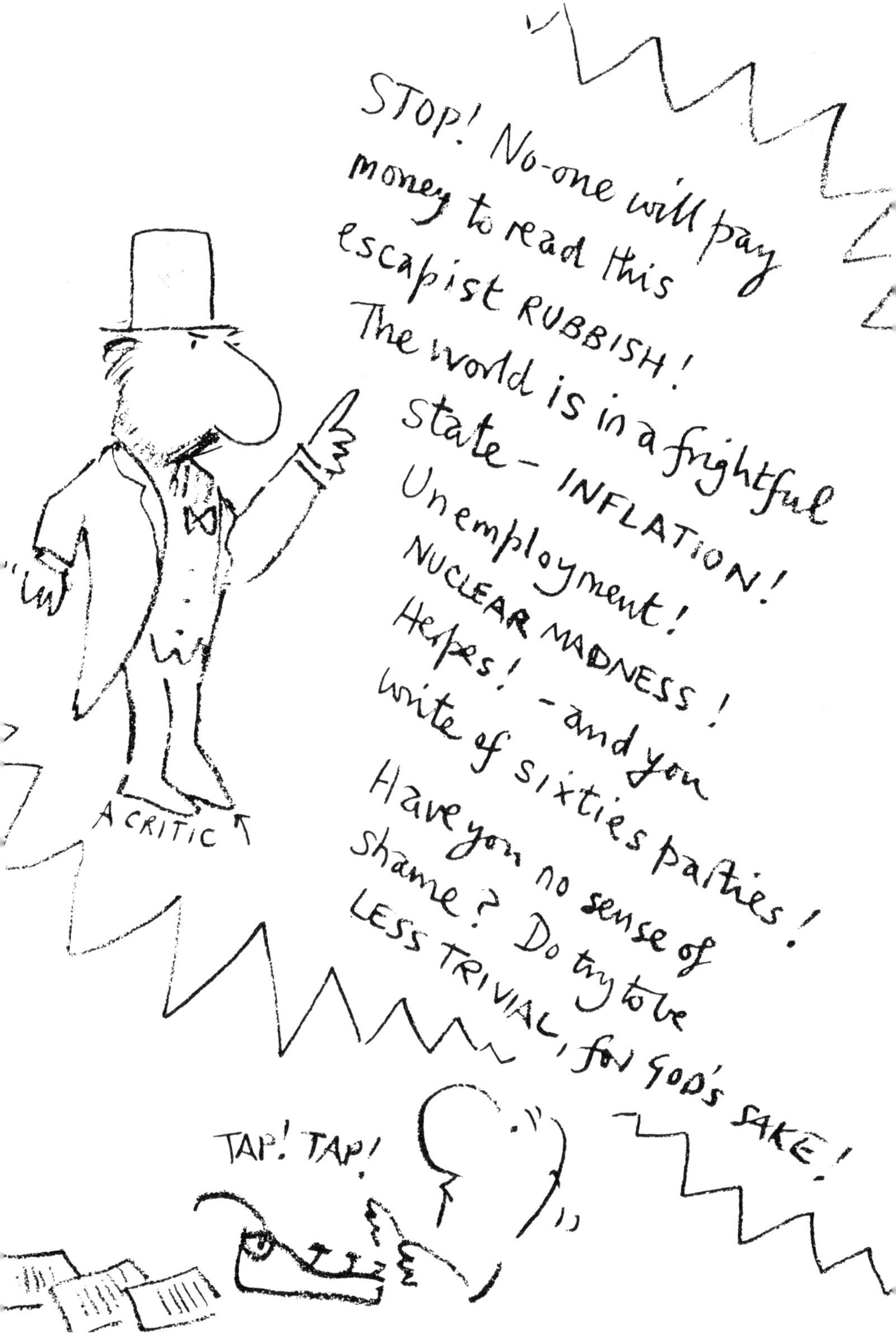

STOP! No-one will pay money to read this escapist RUBBISH! The world is in a frightful state – INFLATION! Unemployment! NUCLEAR MADNESS! Herpes! – and you write of sixties parties! Have you no sense of shame? Do try to be LESS TRIVIAL, for GOD'S SAKE!
A CRITIC
TAP! TAP!

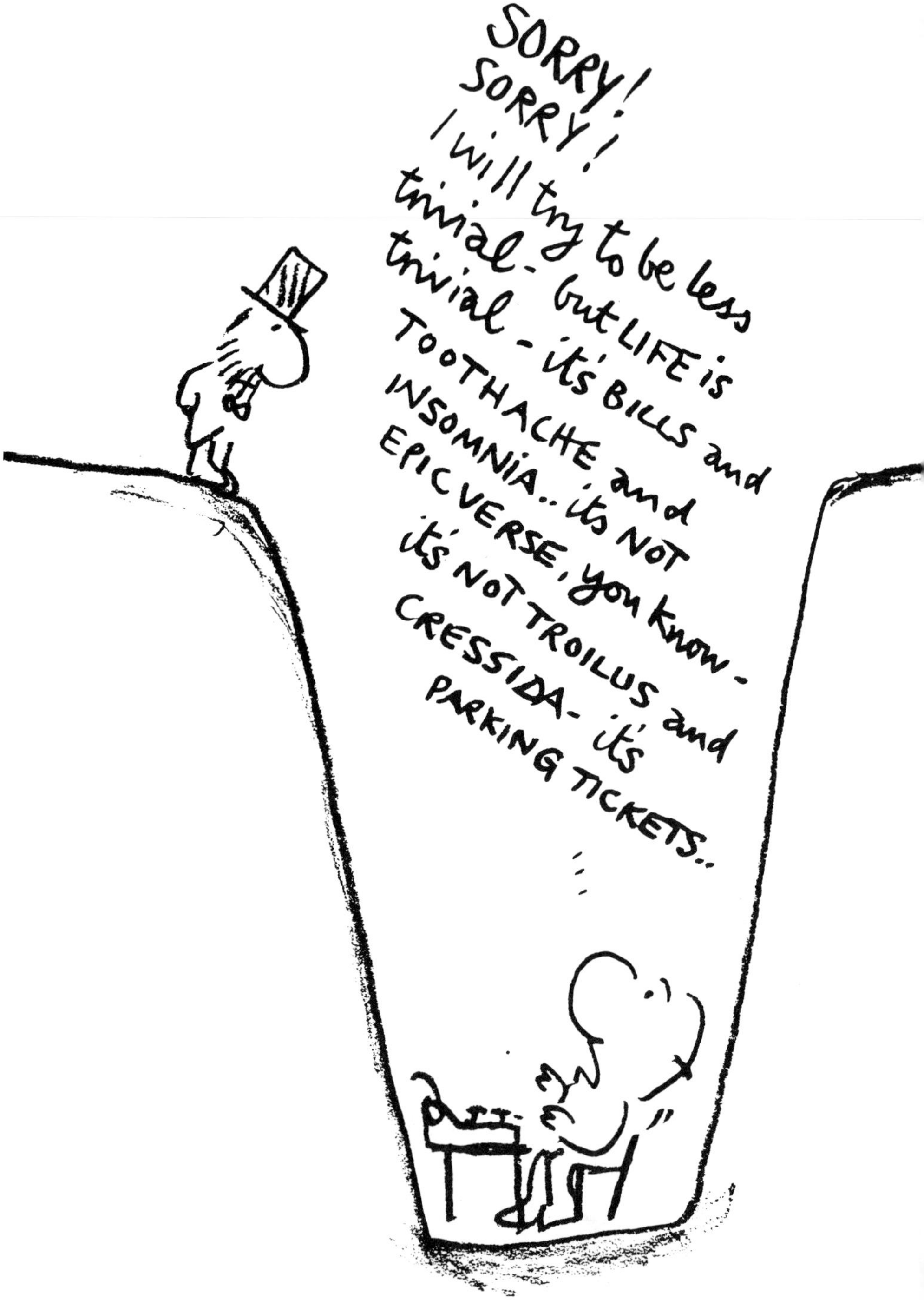
SORRY! SORRY! I will try to be less trivial - but LIFE is trivial - it's BILLS and TOOTHACHE and INSOMNIA.. it's NOT EPIC VERSE, you know - it's NOT TROILUS and CRESSIDA - it's PARKING TICKETS..

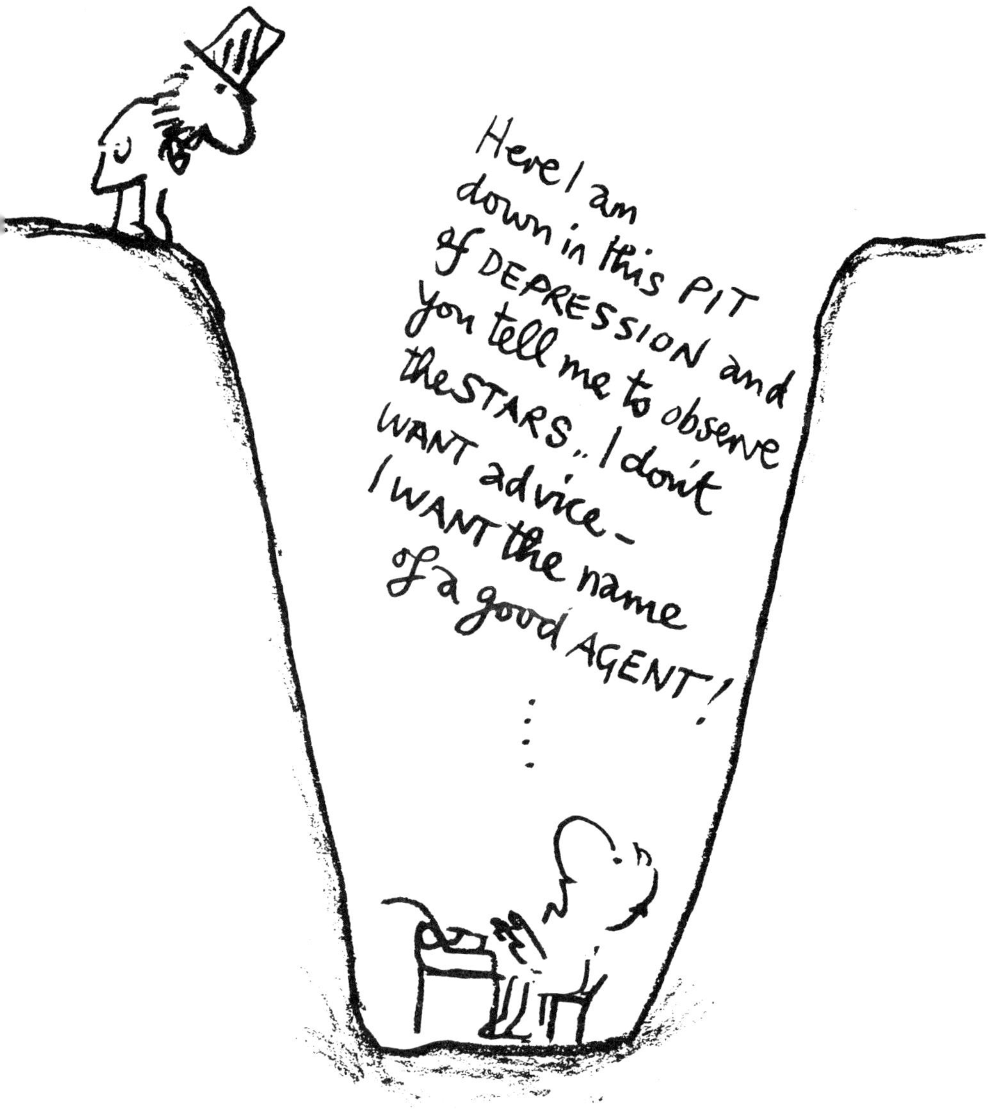
Here I am
down in this PIT
of DEPRESSION and
you tell me to observe
the STARS.. I don't
WANT advice –
I WANT the name
of a good AGENT!
....

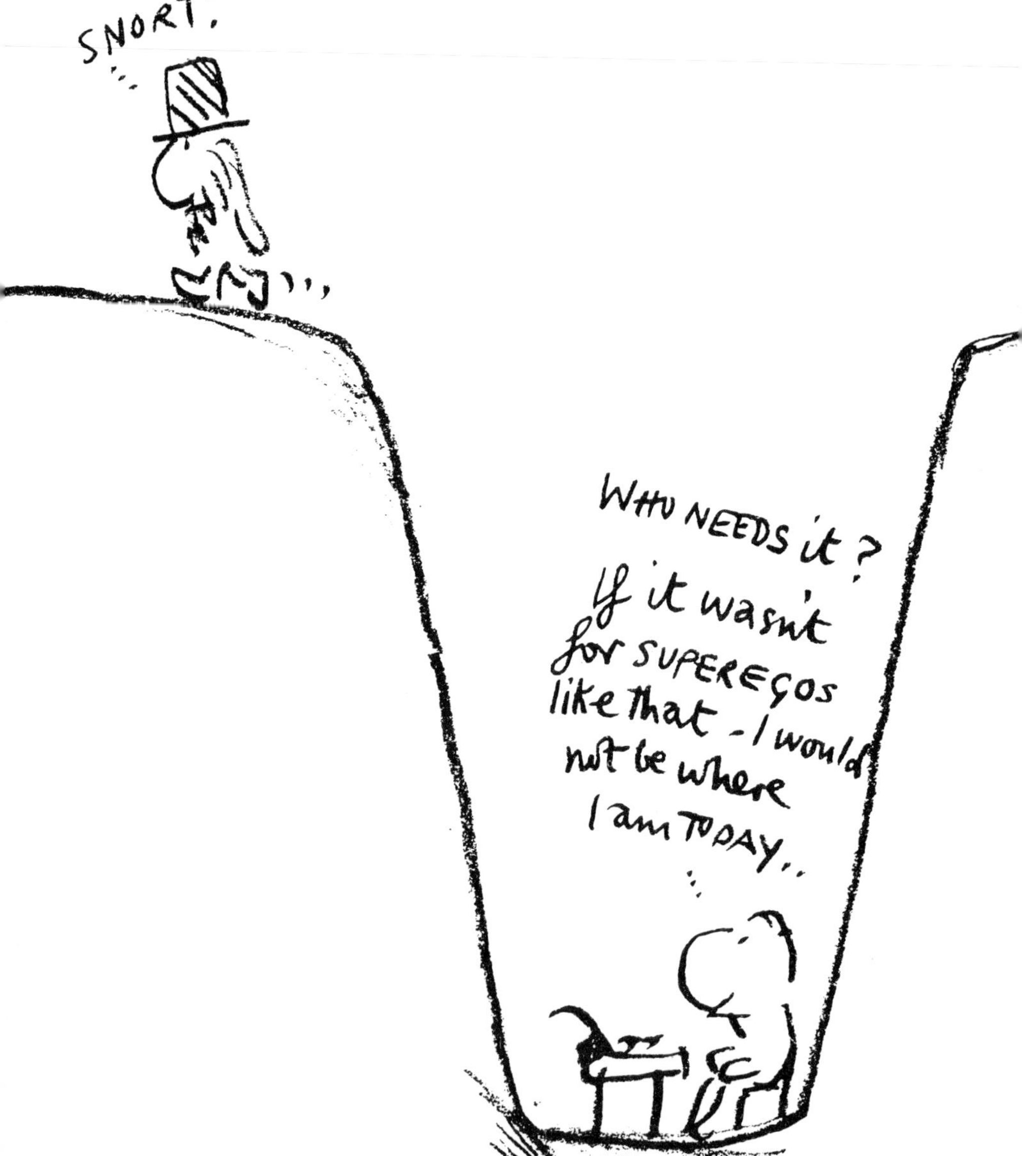
SNORT!
WHO NEEDS it?
If it wasn't for SUPEREGOS like that - I would not be where I am TODAY...

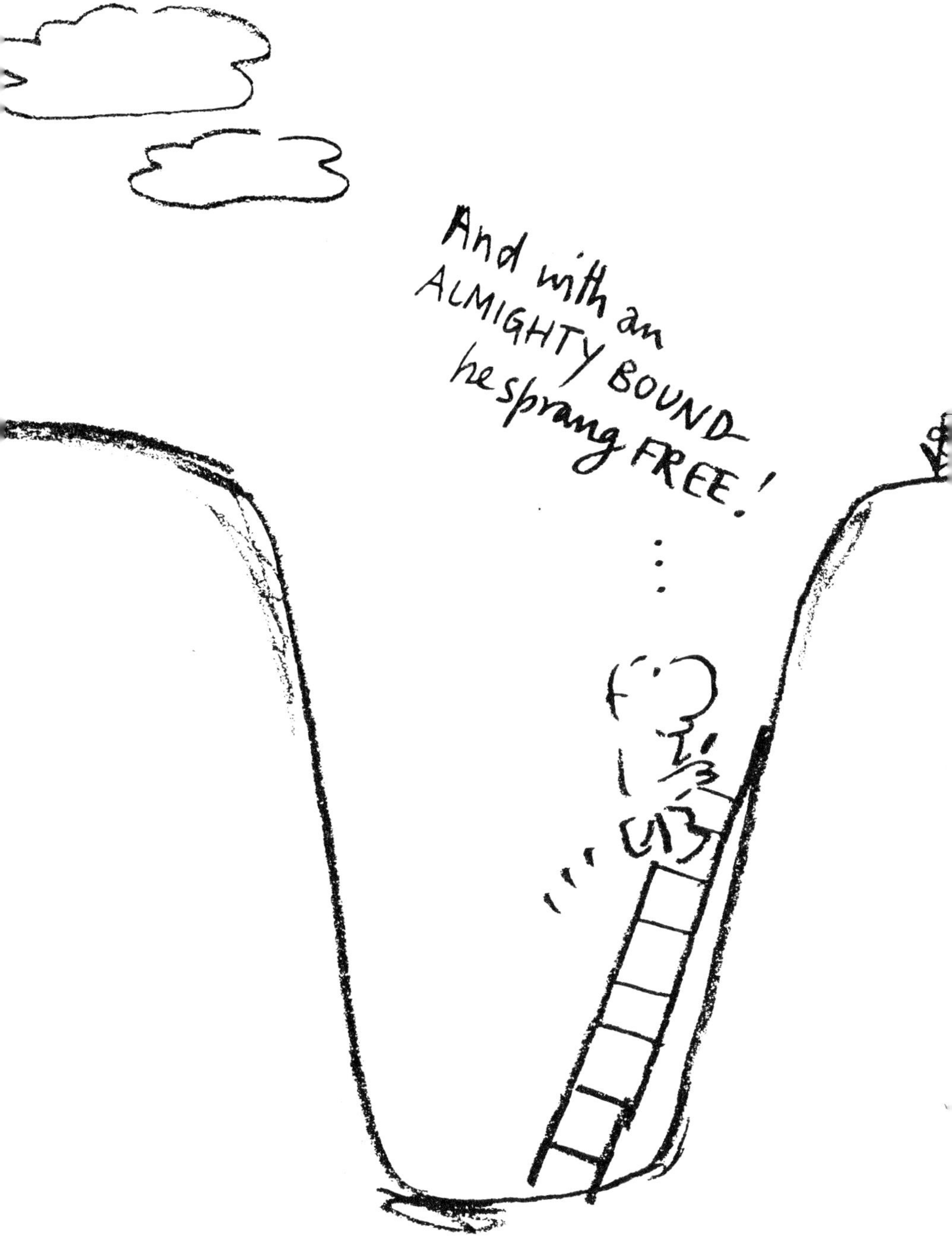
And with an
ALMIGHTY BOUND
he sprang FREE!

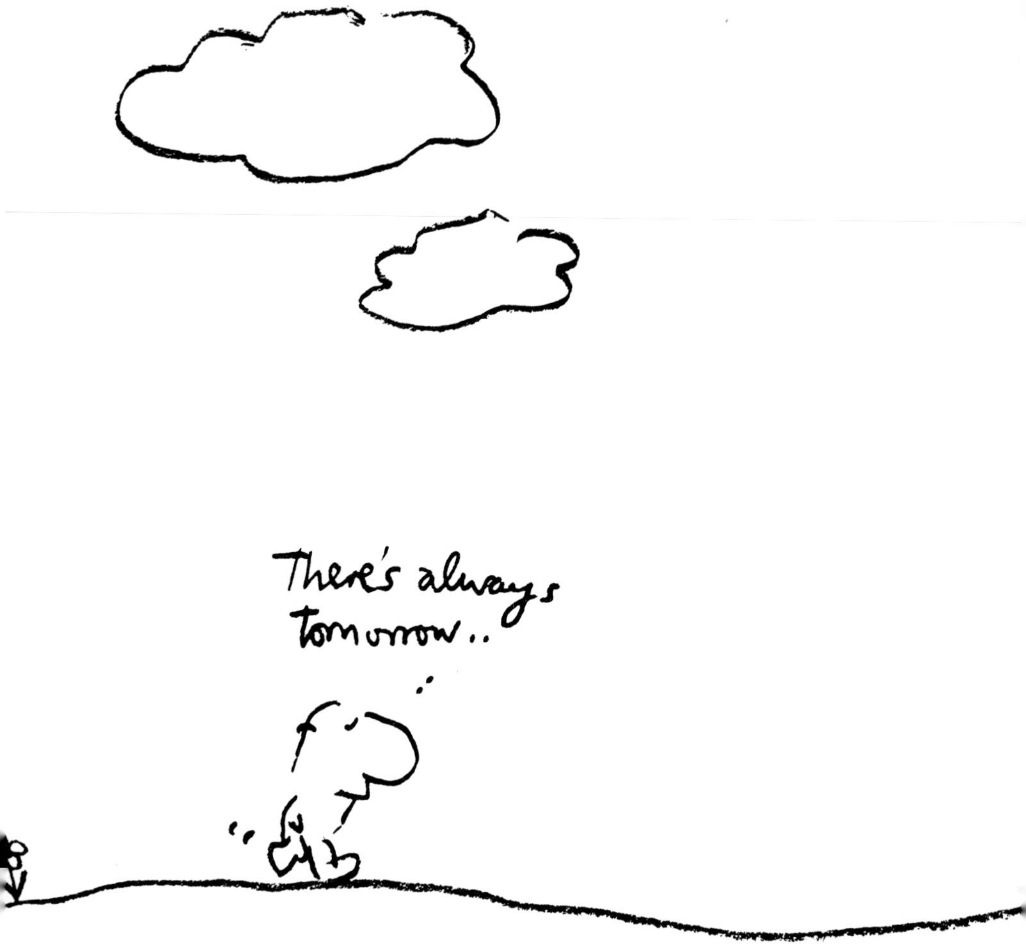
There's always
tomorrow..

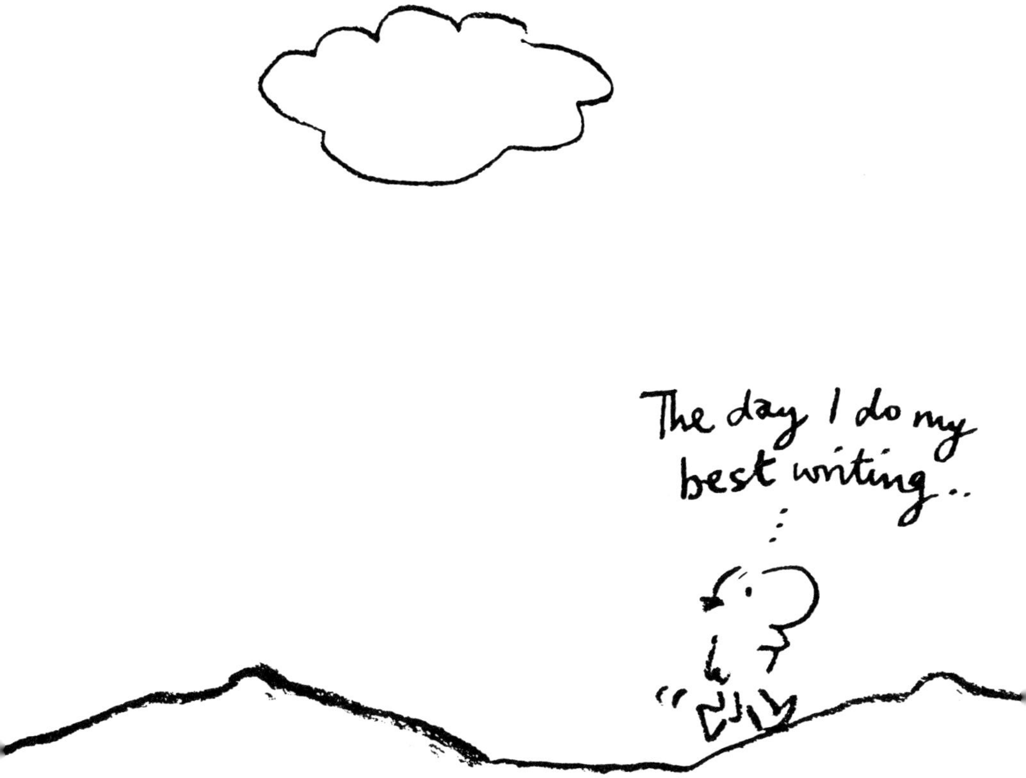
The day I do my best writing..

The NEXT DAY...

I need to discover
who I am before
I can write my BIG NOVEL..
I will visit a WISEMAN..

So he opened the YELLOW PAGES
to see if he could find
a WISE MAN.

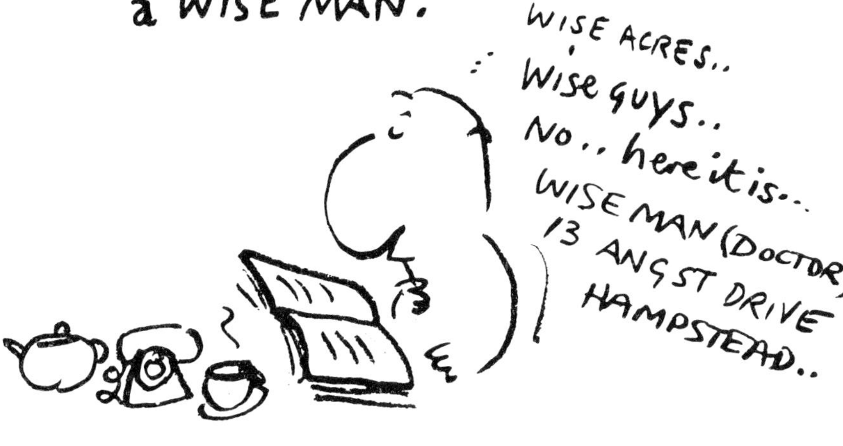
WISE ACRES..
Wise guys..
No.. here it is...
WISE MAN (DOCTOR)
13 ANGST DRIVE
HAMPSTEAD..

As GOLDWYN said -
anyone who sees a shrink
needs their head examined..

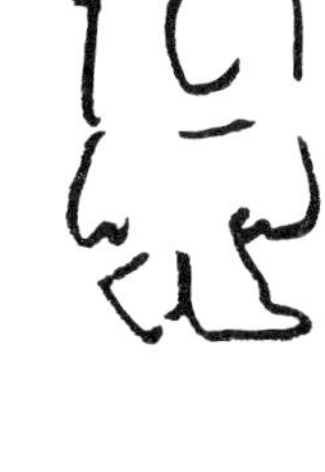

An appointment is made
and the following MONDAY...
he sits facing DR. WISEMAN..

So - what's
the problem?
Lie down
and relax..

I don't want
to RELAX —
I feel too TENSE
to relax!

:

I want to know
who I am –
why I am –
and when will it get better –
and if NOT
Why NOT?

. :
.

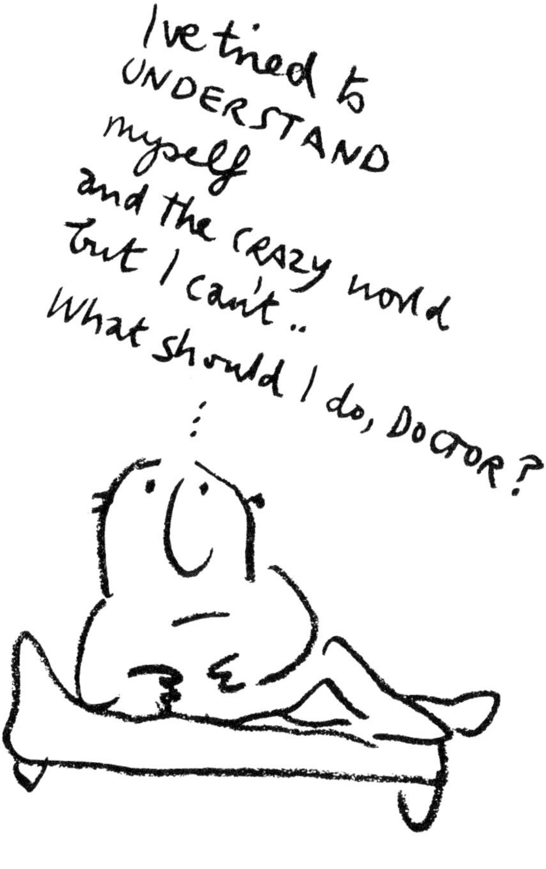
Ive tried to
UNDERSTAND
myself
and the CRAZY world
but I can't..
What should I do, DOCTOR?

The DOCTOR
thinks..

Mm.. mm..
Probably OEDIPAL..
with NEGATIVE TRANSFERENCE..
even ANAL RETENTIVE..
certainly SCHIZOID.. with
a touch of SHOE FETISHISM..
fascinating..
WONDERFUL..

The DOCTOR
Speaks...

Come and see me
for a little while..
Say twice a week
(for ten years)
while we discover
the REAL PROBLEM..
we need to get to the
ROOTS of the difficulties..
So TILL NEXT WEEK—

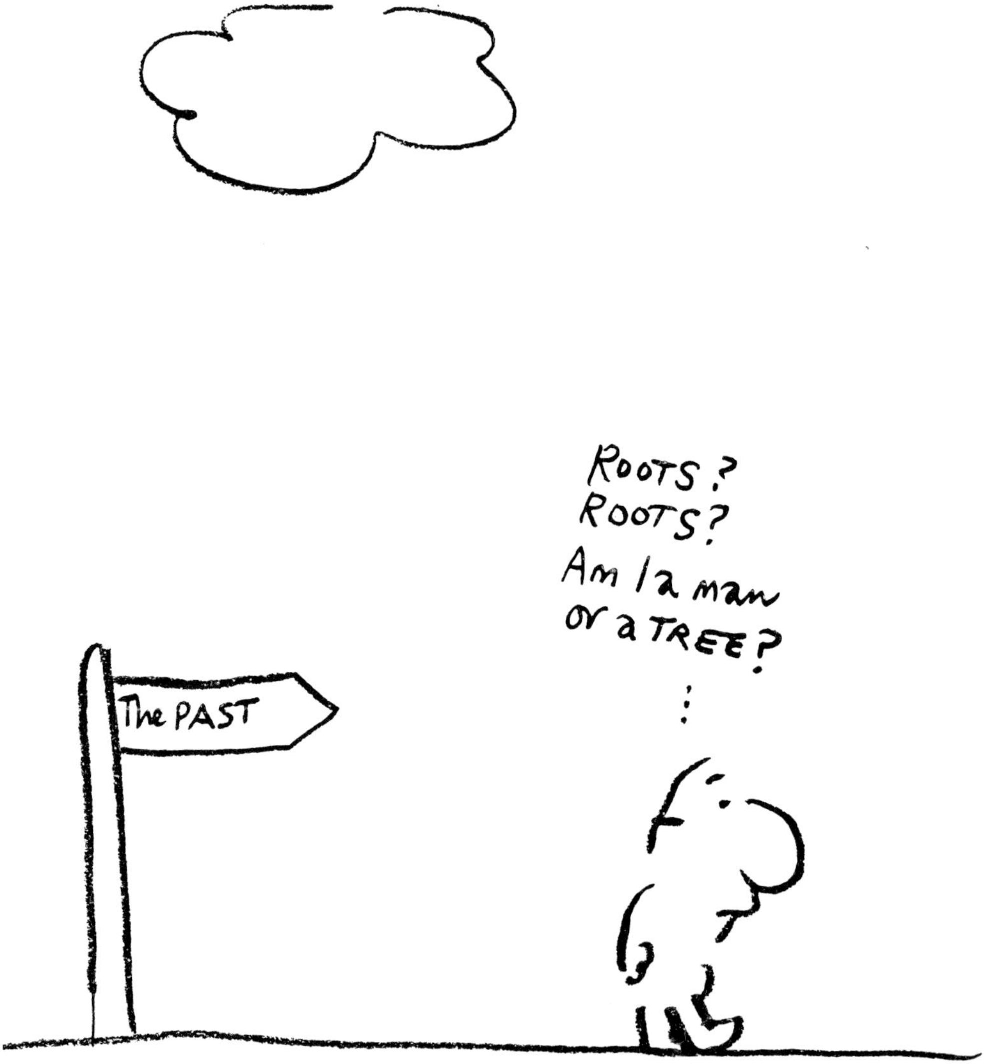
ROOTS?
ROOTS?
Am I a man
or a TREE?
The PAST

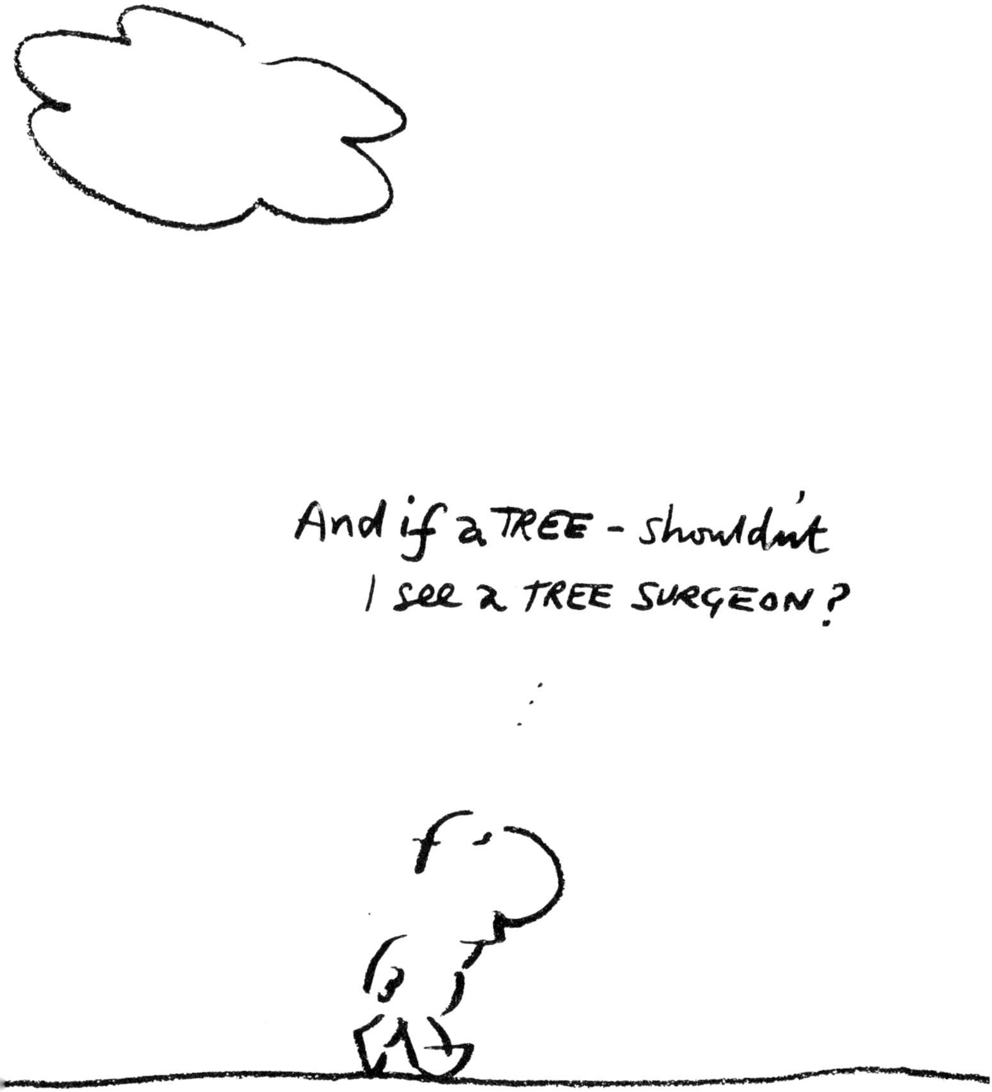
And if a TREE - shouldn't
I see a TREE SURGEON?

Meawhile-
The WORLD
continued spinning..

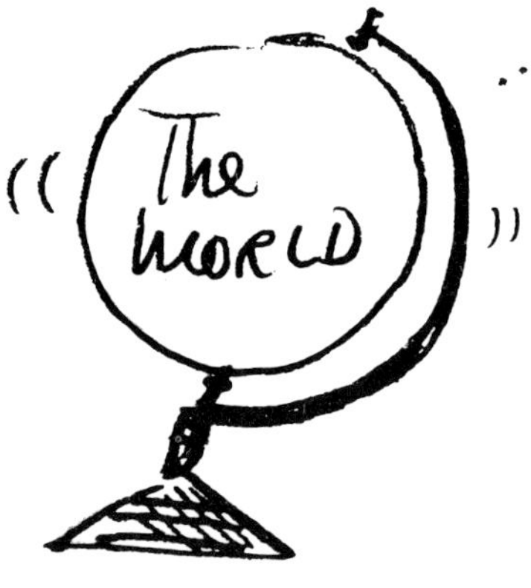
We just lost POLAND, MR PRESIDENT
Well- let's try for another TAKE!
The WORLD

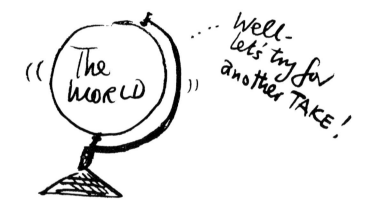

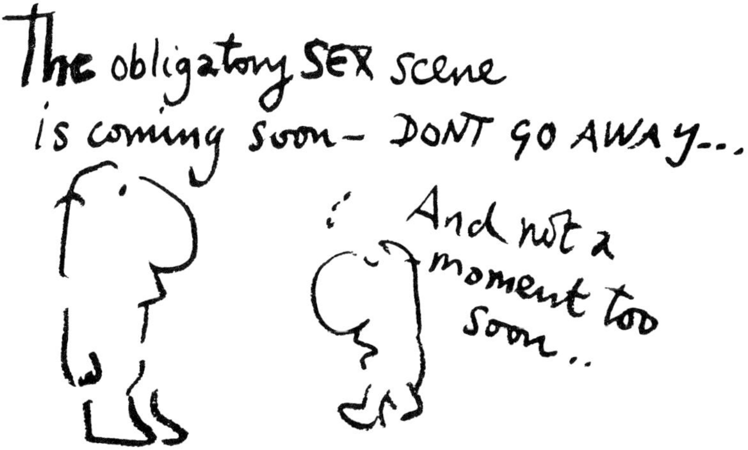
The obligatory SEX scene
is coming soon – DONT GO AWAY...
And not a
moment too
soon..

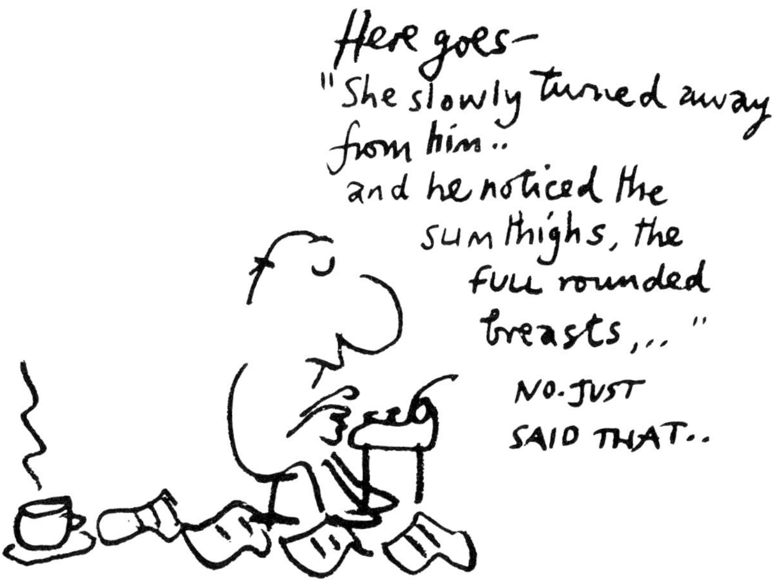
Here goes –
"She slowly turned away
from him..
and he noticed the
slim thighs, the
full rounded
breasts,.."
NO. JUST
SAID THAT..

If I'm reduced to writing SOFT PORN -
I certainly need a holiday..

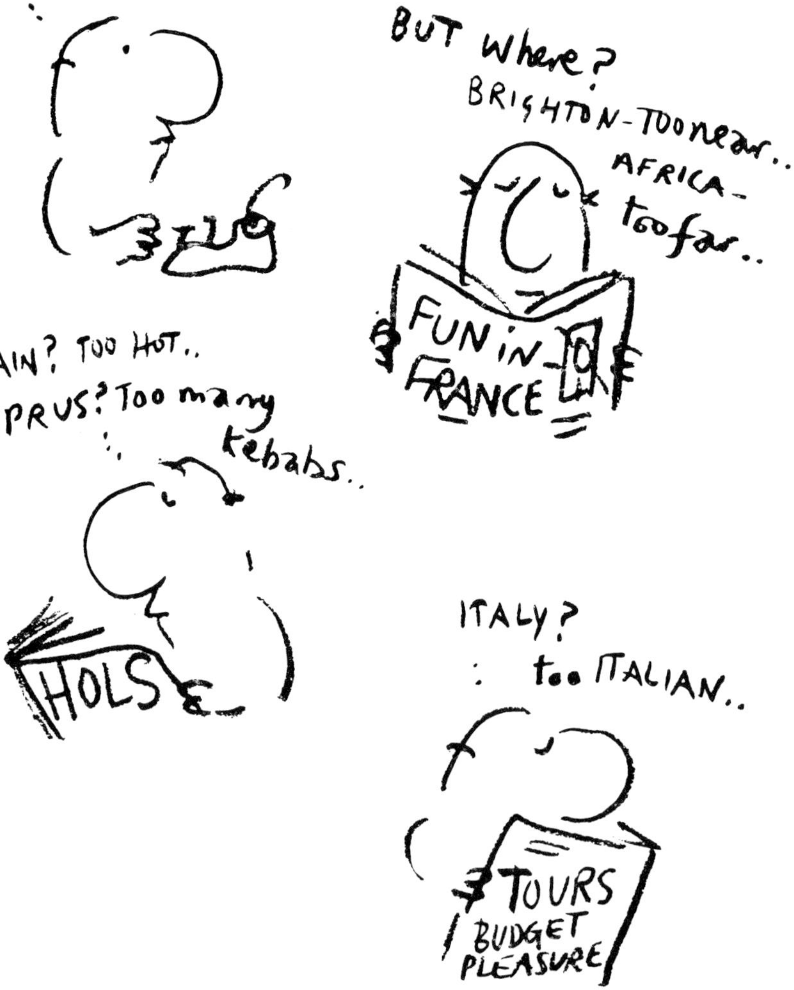
BUT Where?
BRIGHTON - TOO near..
AFRICA - too far..
FUN IN FRANCE
SPAIN? TOO HOT..
CYPRUS? Too many kebabs..
HOLS
ITALY? too ITALIAN..
TOURS
BUDGET PLEASURE

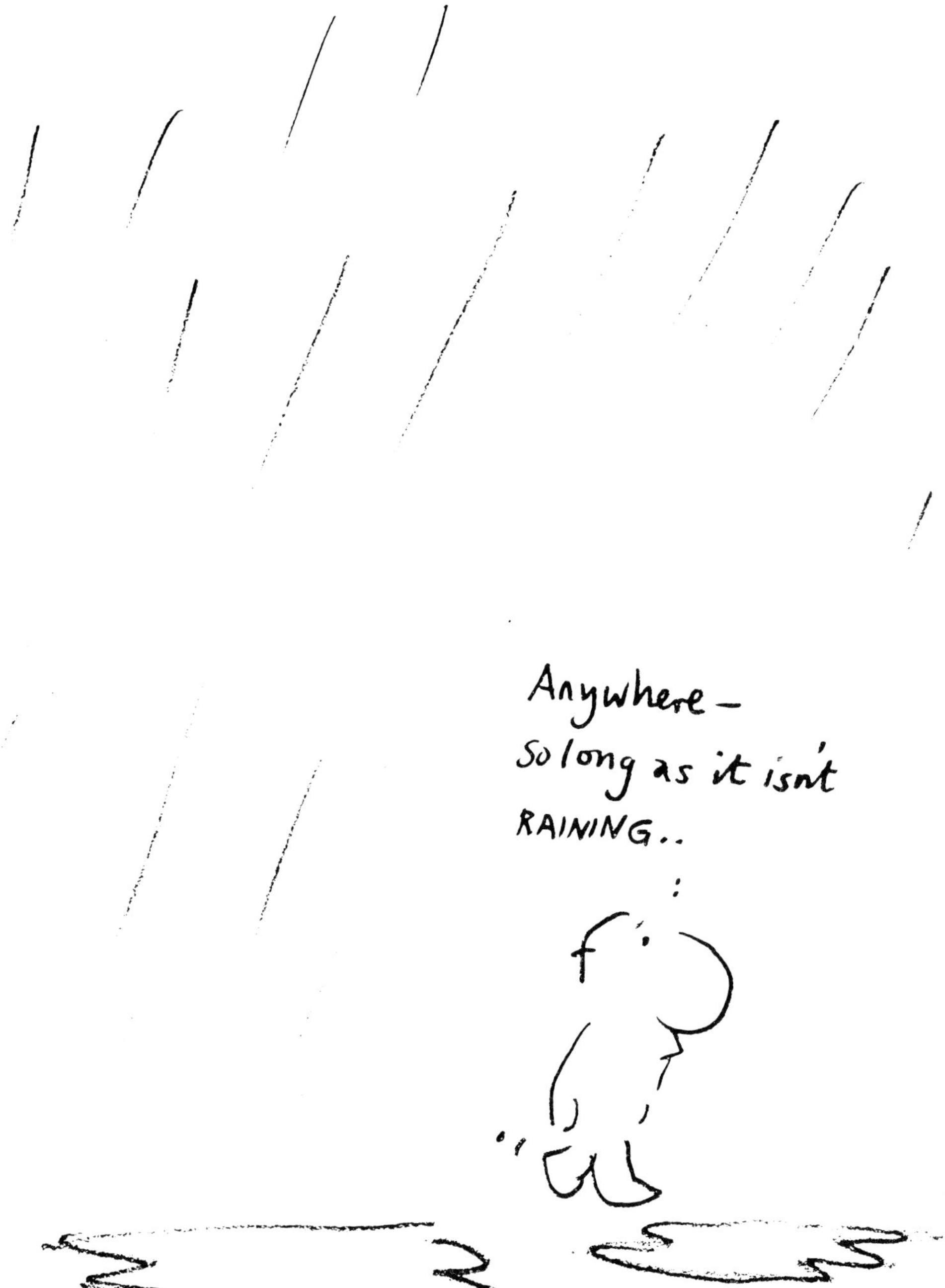
Anywhere –
So long as it isn't
RAINING..

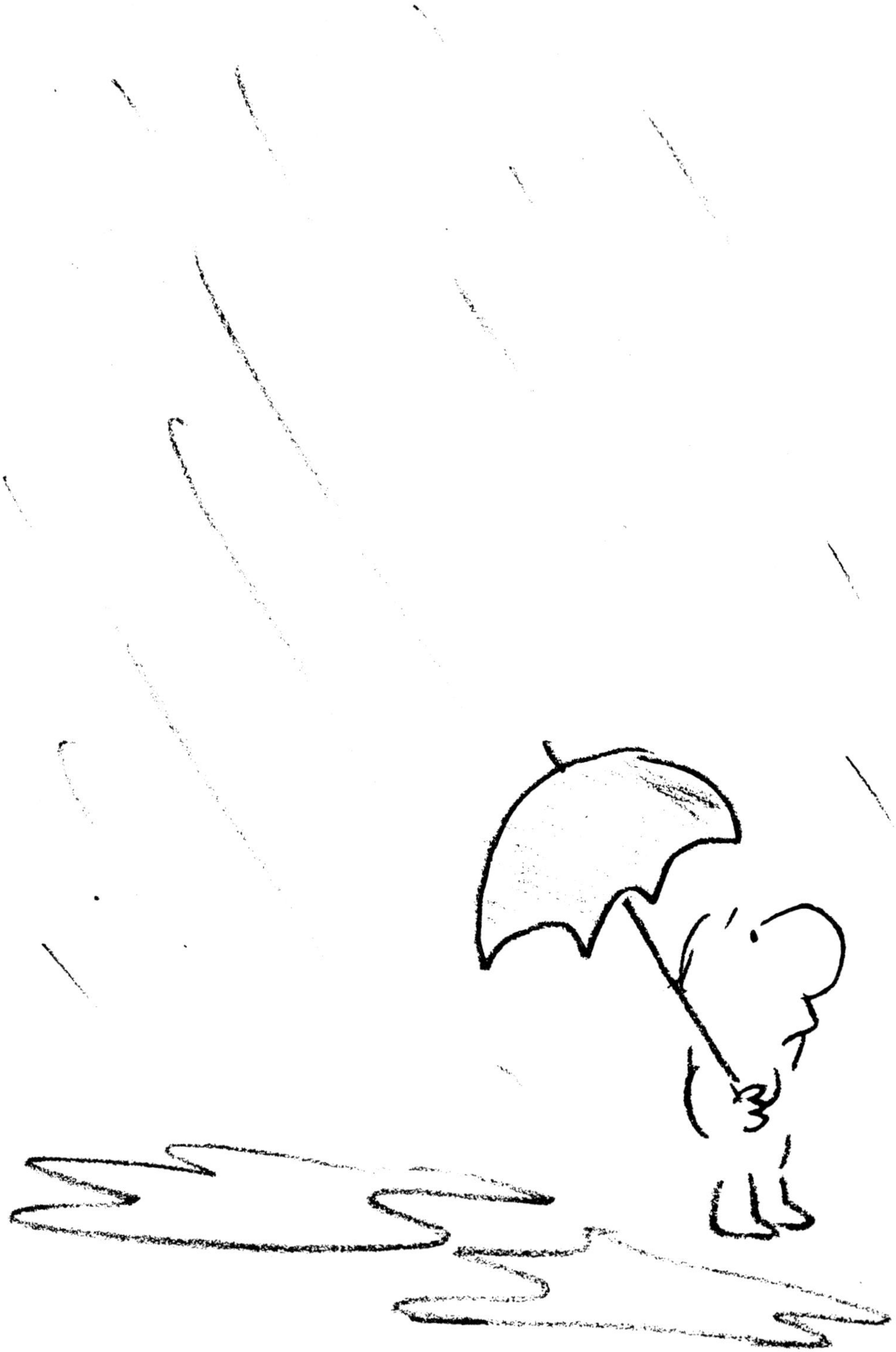

So he cancelled all his
appointments (both of them)
and went to PARIS.
In PARIS it was raining..

it's a very
DAMP
moveable
FEAST...

He unpacked his case
and went to eat in a nearby BISTRO...

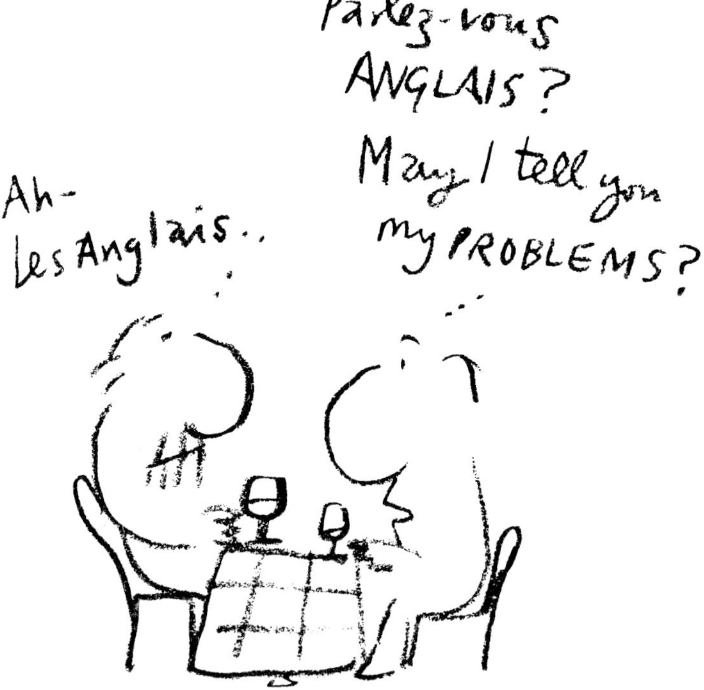
Parlez-vous ANGLAIS? May I tell you my PROBLEMS?
Ah- les Anglais..

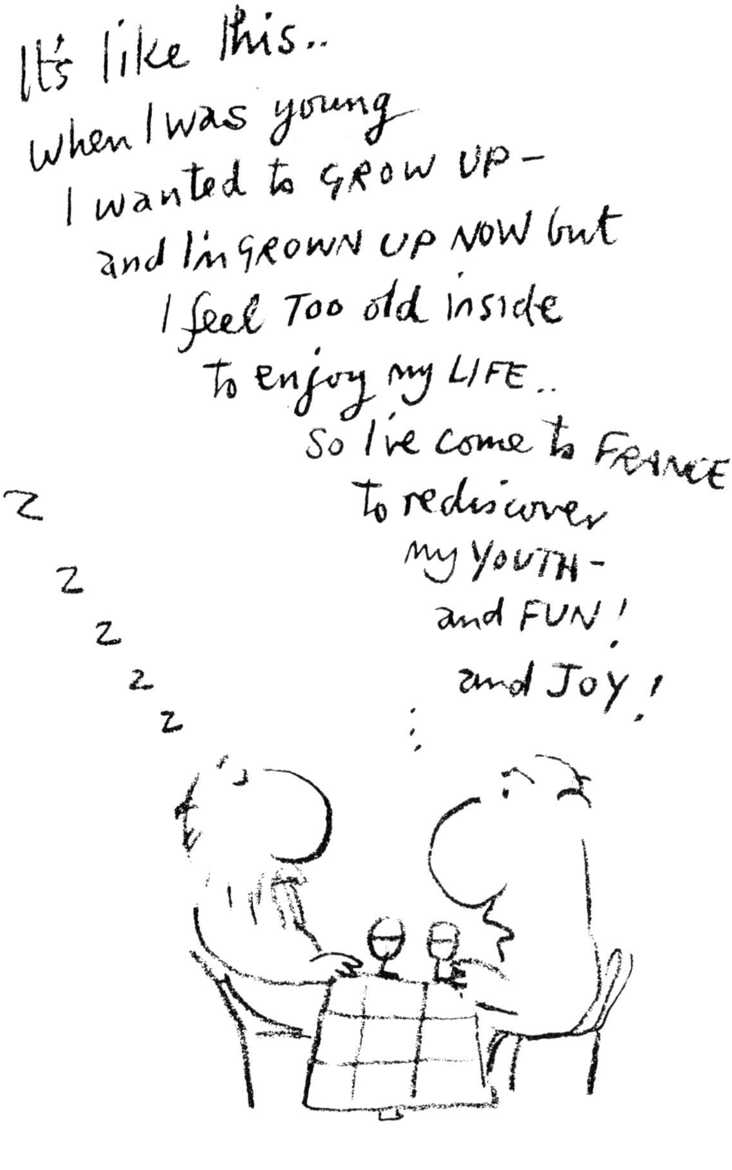
It's like this..
when I was young
I wanted to GROW UP -
and I'm GROWN UP NOW but
I feel TOO old inside
to enjoy my LIFE..
So I've come to FRANCE
to rediscover
my YOUTH -
and FUN!
and JOY!
Z Z Z Z Z

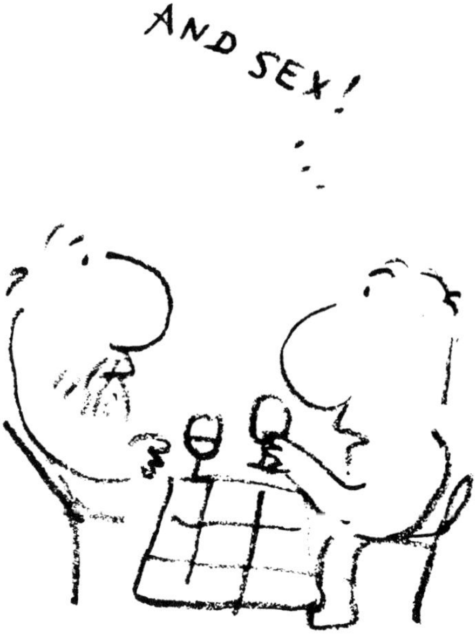
AND SEX! ...

The FRENCHMAN WAKES UP!

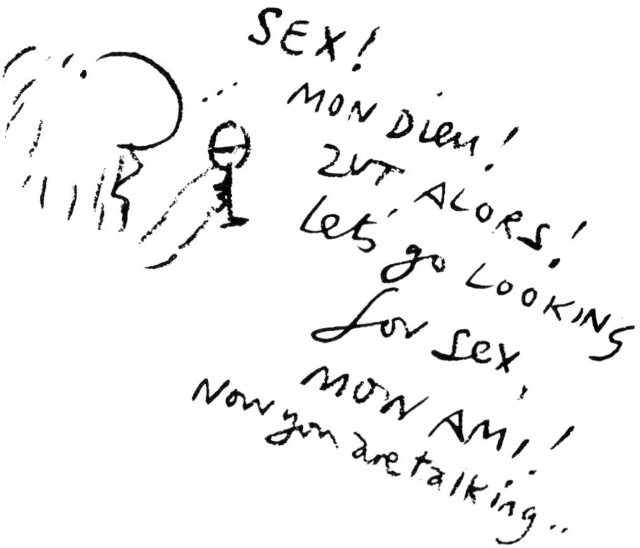
SEX!
MON DIEU!
ZUT ALORS!
Let's go LOOKING for sex MON AMI!
Now you are talking..

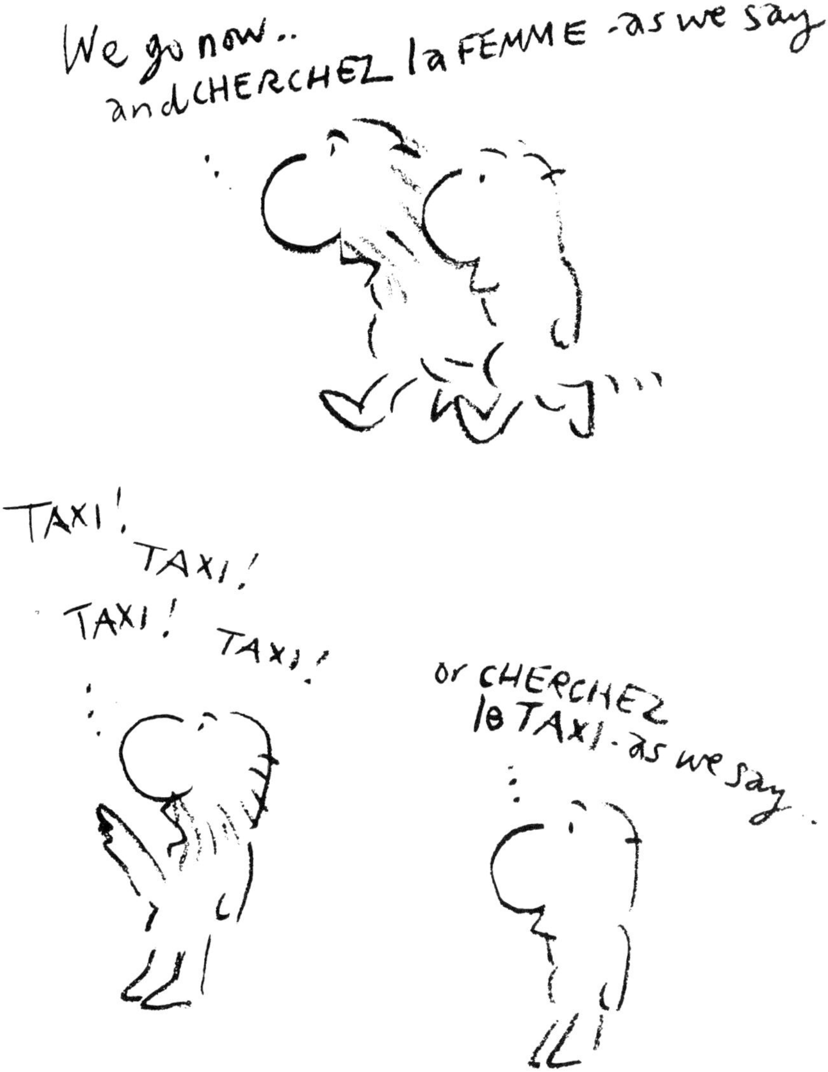
We go now.. and CHERCHEZ la FEMME - as we say
TAXI! TAXI! TAXI! TAXI!
or CHERCHEZ le TAXI - as we say..

They stop near Les Halles
and walk along a NARROW STREET..

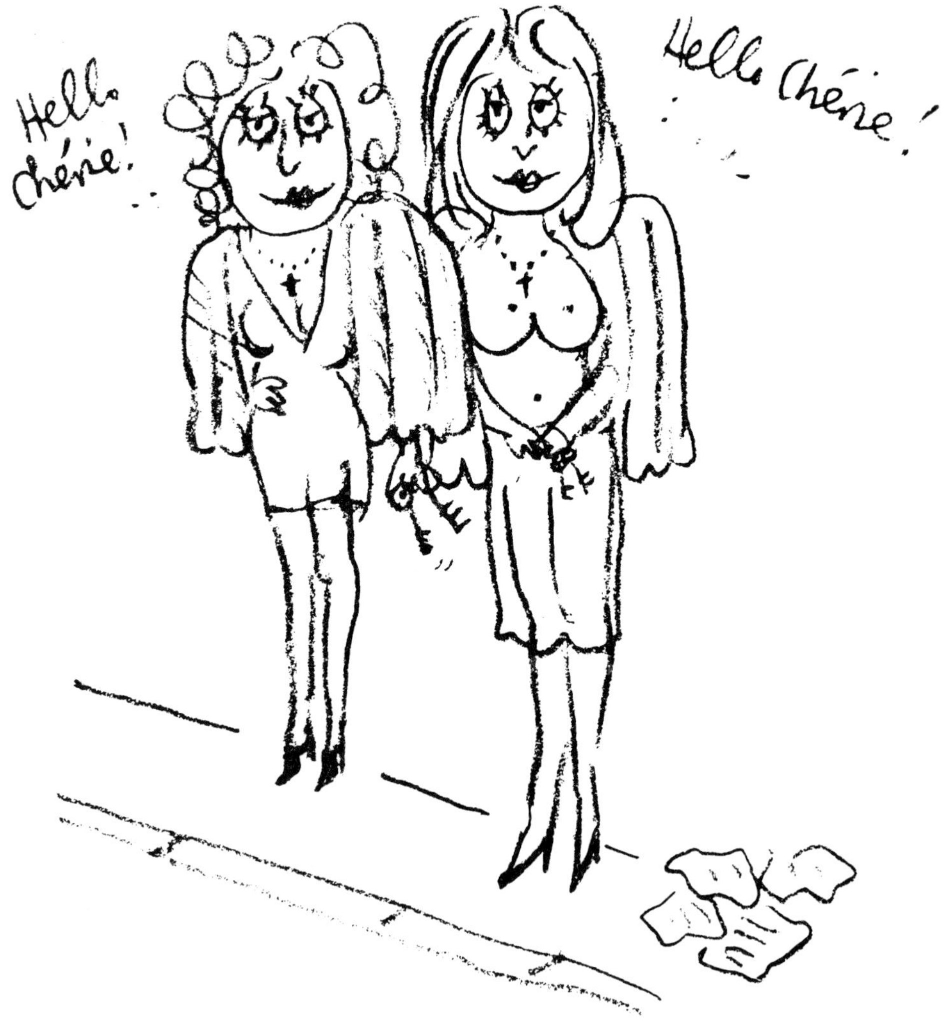
Hello chérie!
Hello Chérie!

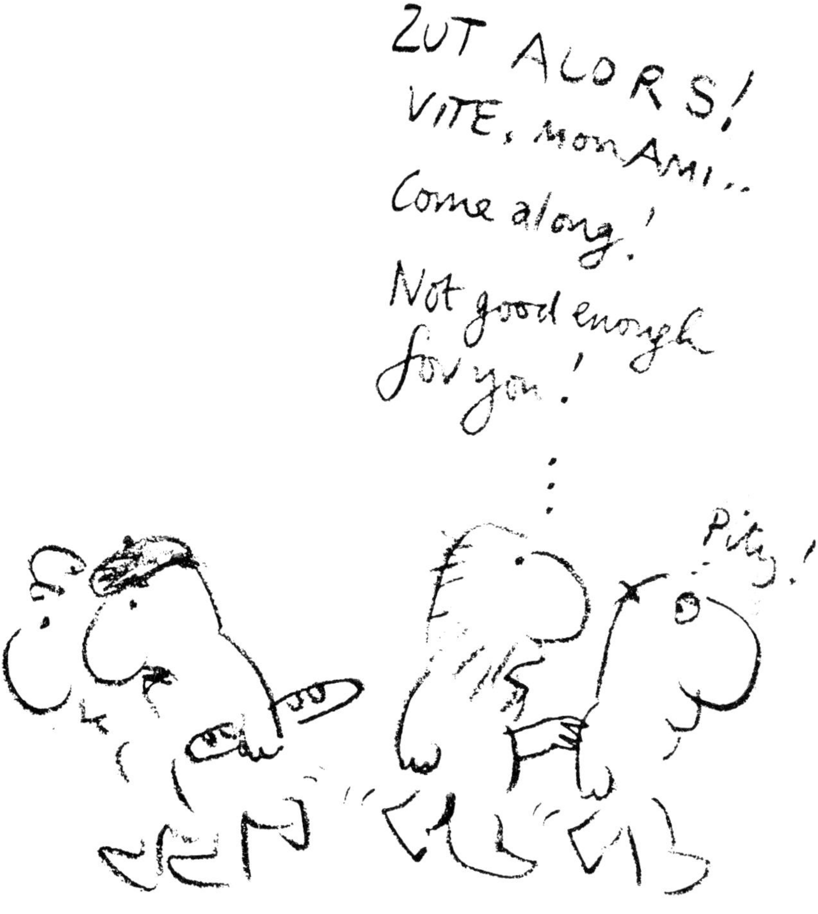
ZUT ALORS!
VITE, MON AMI...
Come along!
Not good enough for you!
...
Pity!

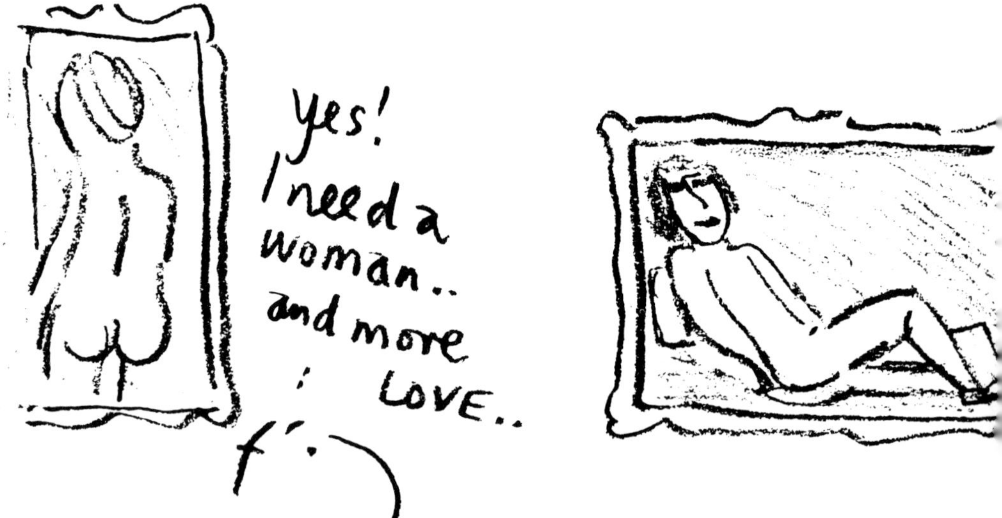
Yes!
I need a
woman..
and more
LOVE..

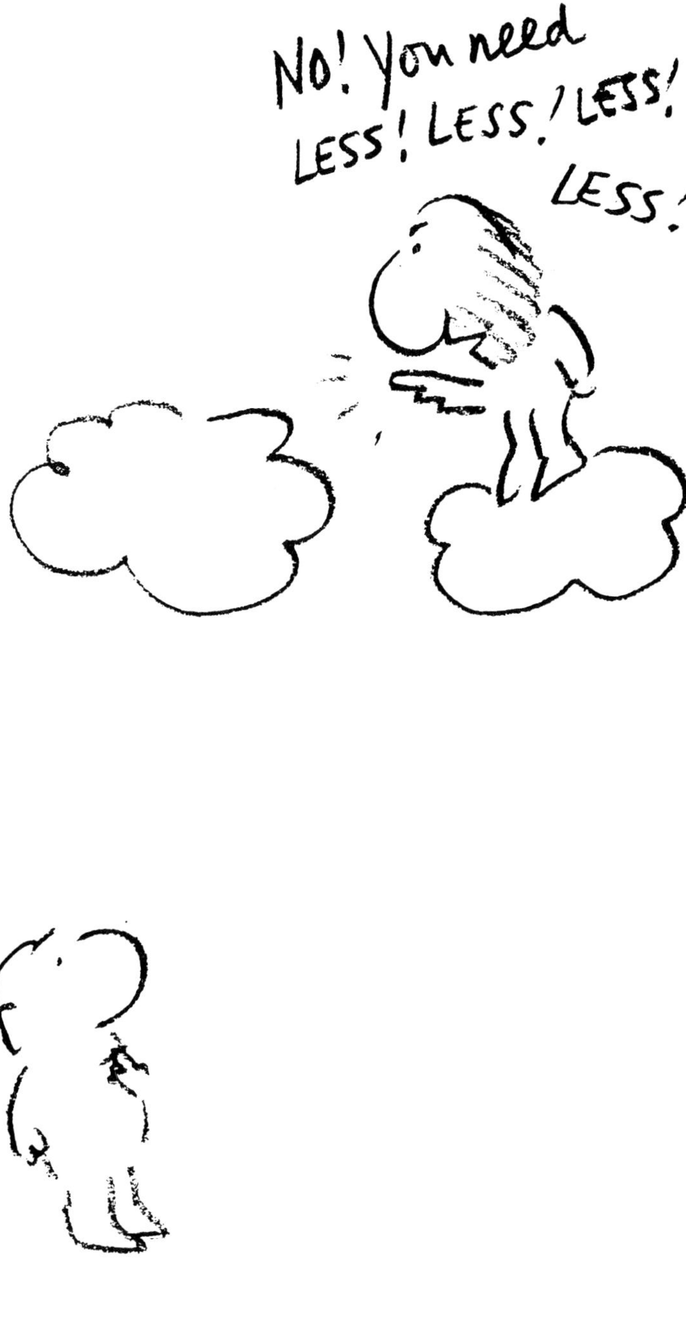
No! You need
LESS! LESS! LESS!
LESS!

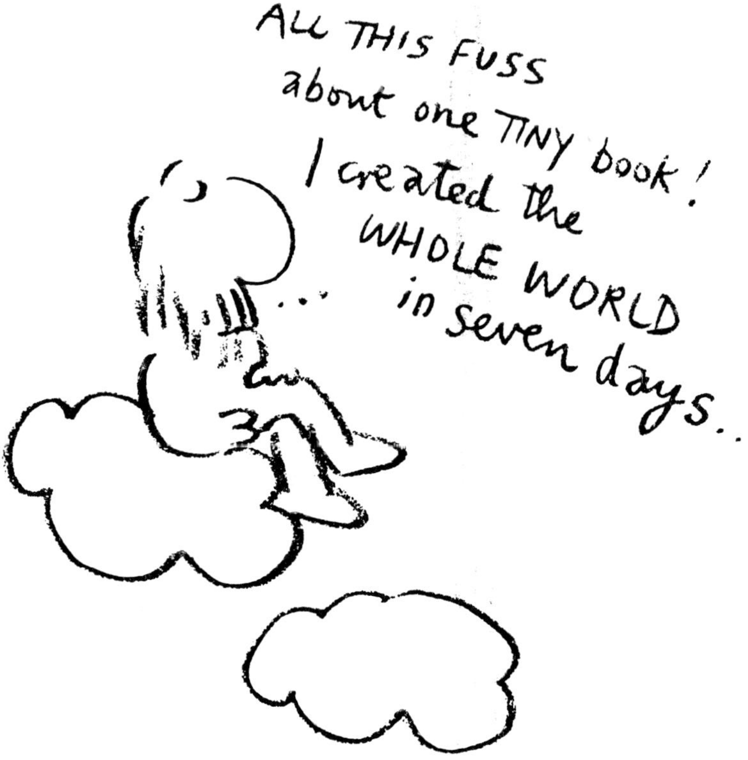
ALL THIS FUSS
about one TINY book!
I created the
WHOLE WORLD
in seven days...

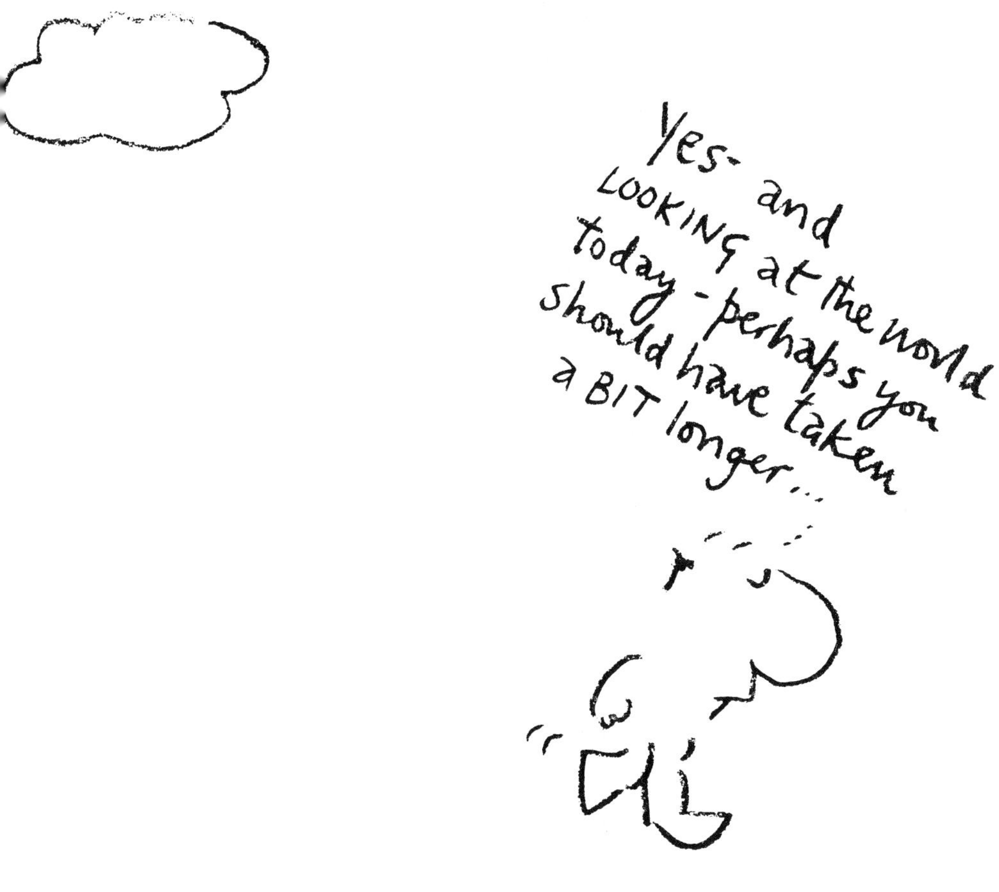
Yes- and
LOOKING at the world
today - perhaps you
should have taken
a BIT longer...

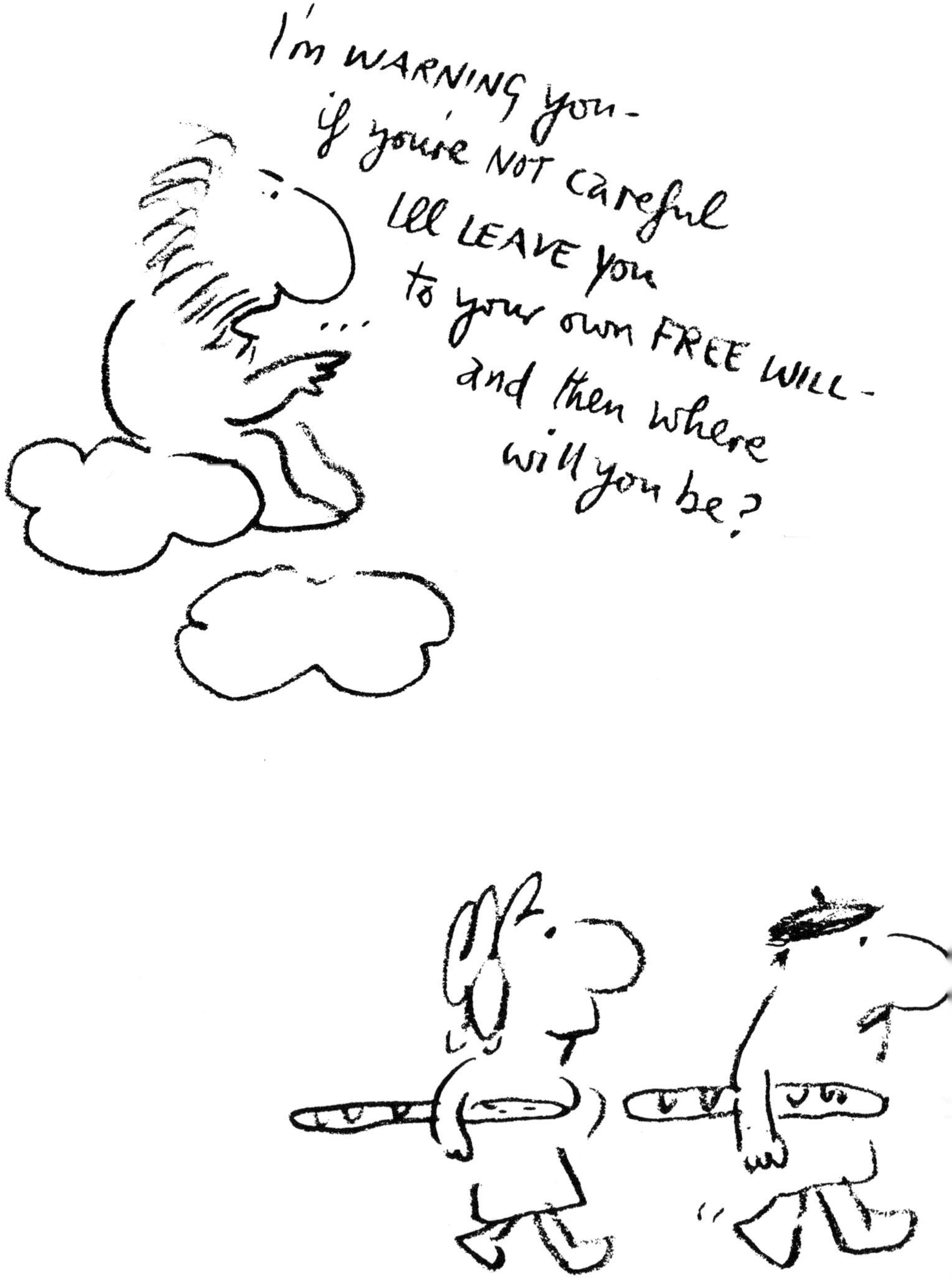
I'm WARNING you - if you're NOT careful I'll LEAVE you to your own FREE WILL - and then where will you be?

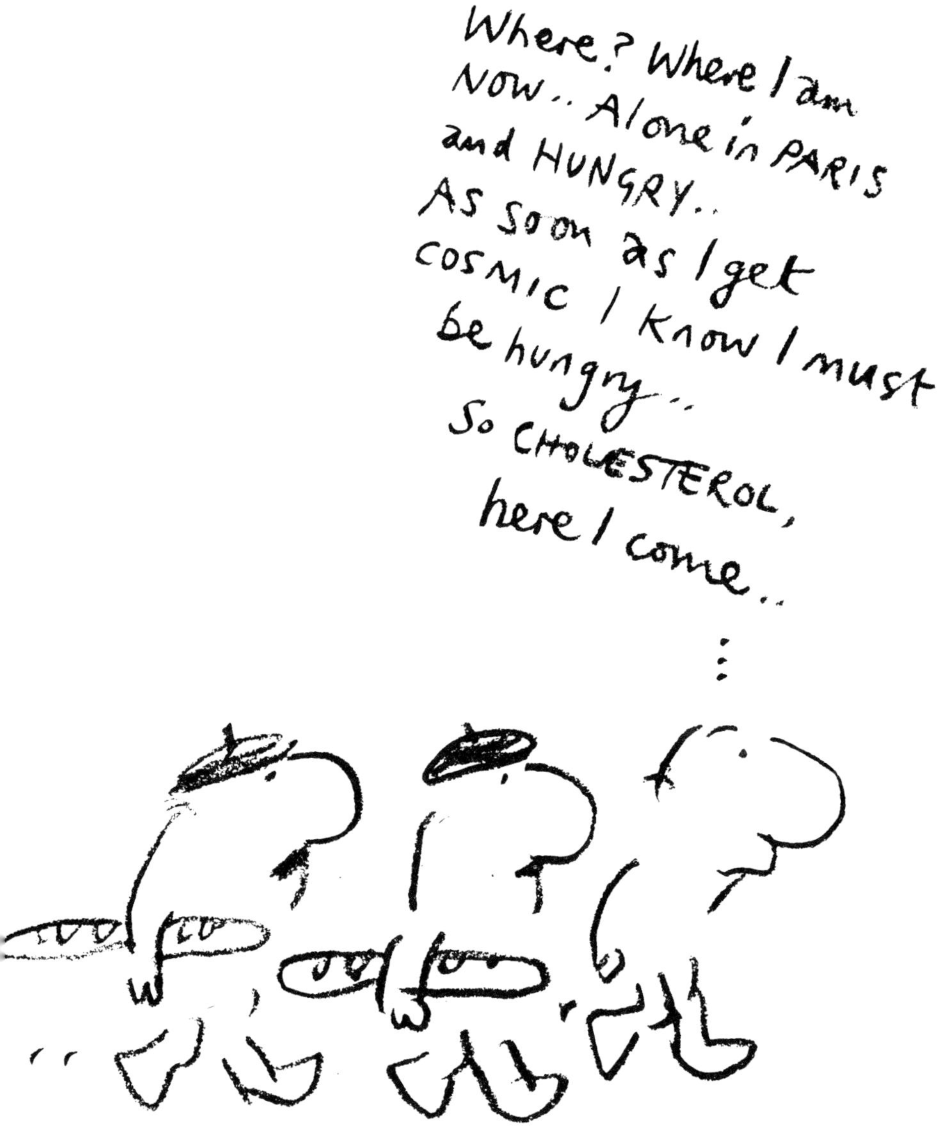
Where? Where I am NOW.. Alone in PARIS and HUNGRY.. As soon as I get COSMIC I know I must be hungry.. So CHOLESTEROL, here I come..

After a splendid DINNER
followed by too many COGNACS,
he dreamed that he had
finished his NOVEL ...

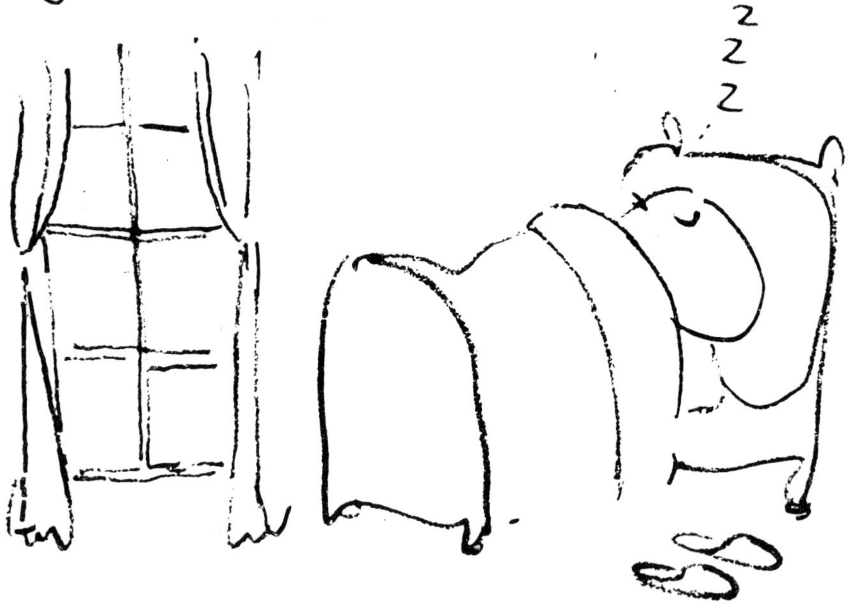
Z
Z
Z

But when he woke up -
he couldn't remember
how it ENDED..

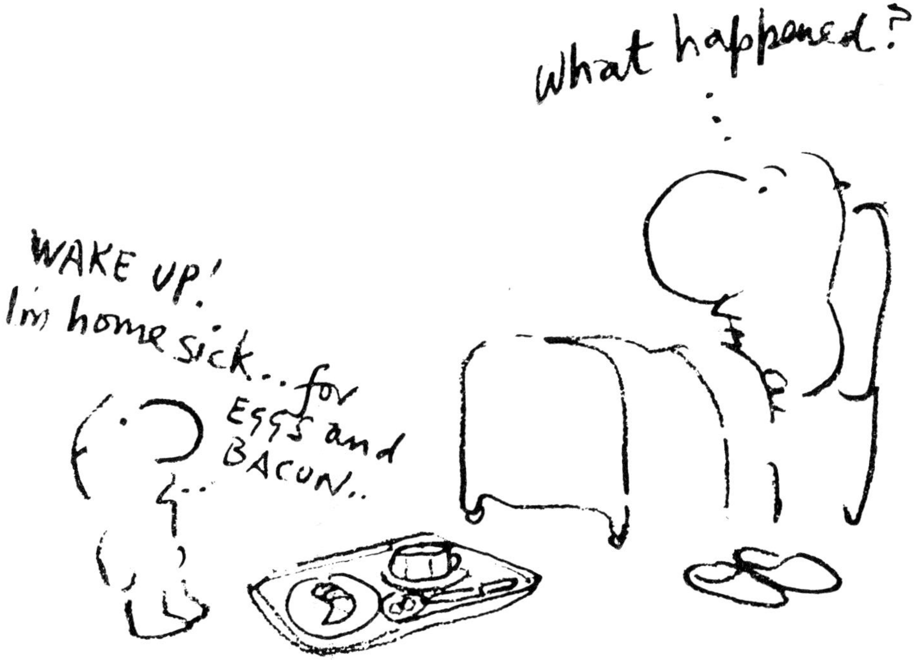
What happened?
WAKE UP!
I'm home sick..for EGGS and BACON..

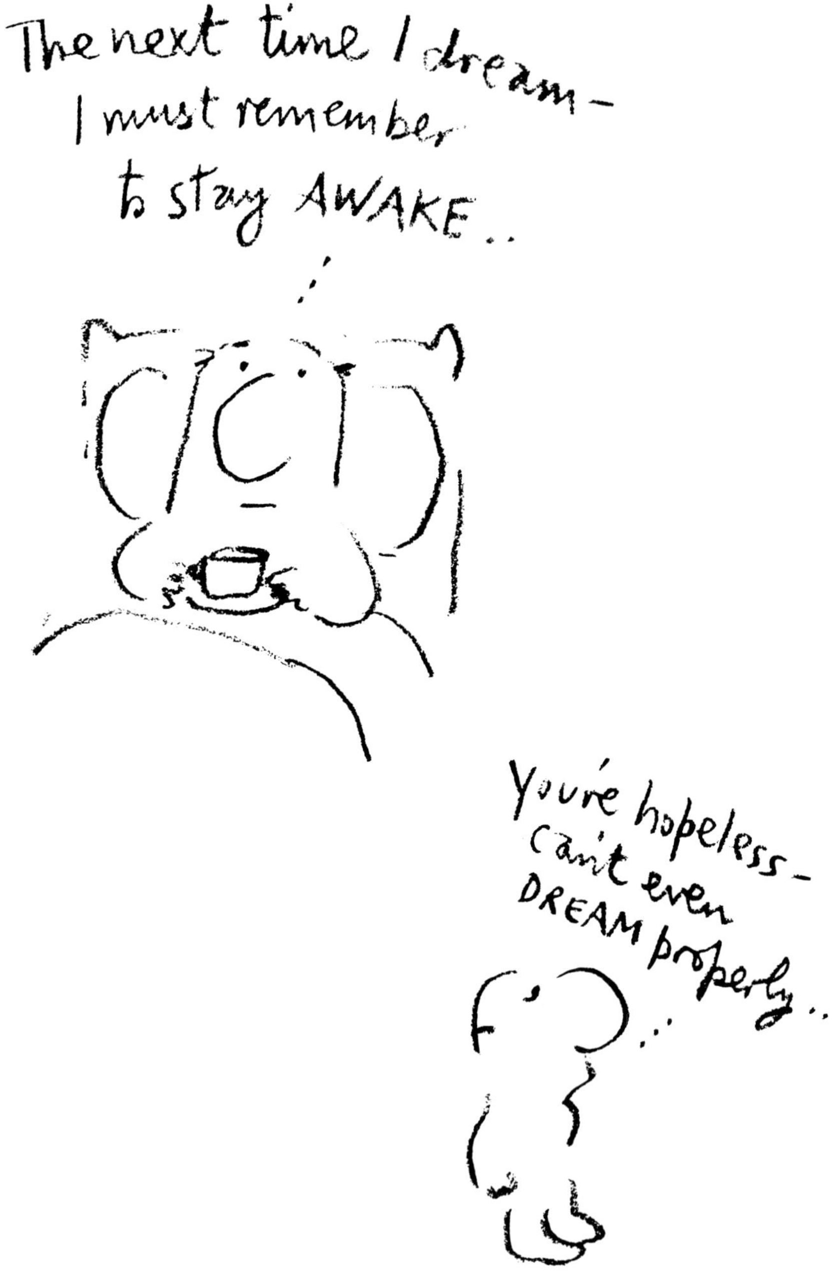
The next time I dream-
I must remember
to stay AWAKE..
You're hopeless-
can't even
DREAM properly..

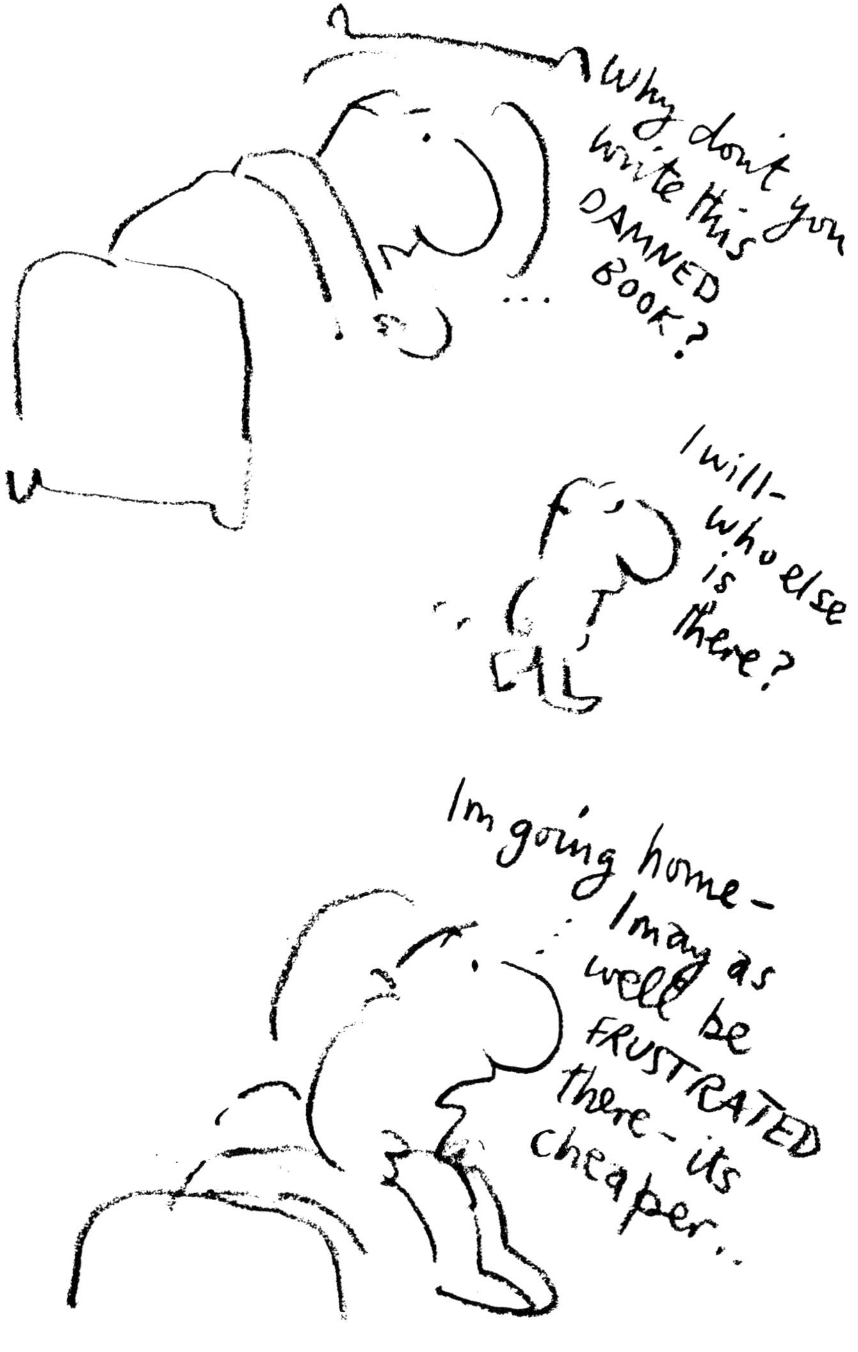
Why don't you write this DAMNED BOOK?
I will - who else is there?
I'm going home - I may as well be FRUSTRATED there - its cheaper..

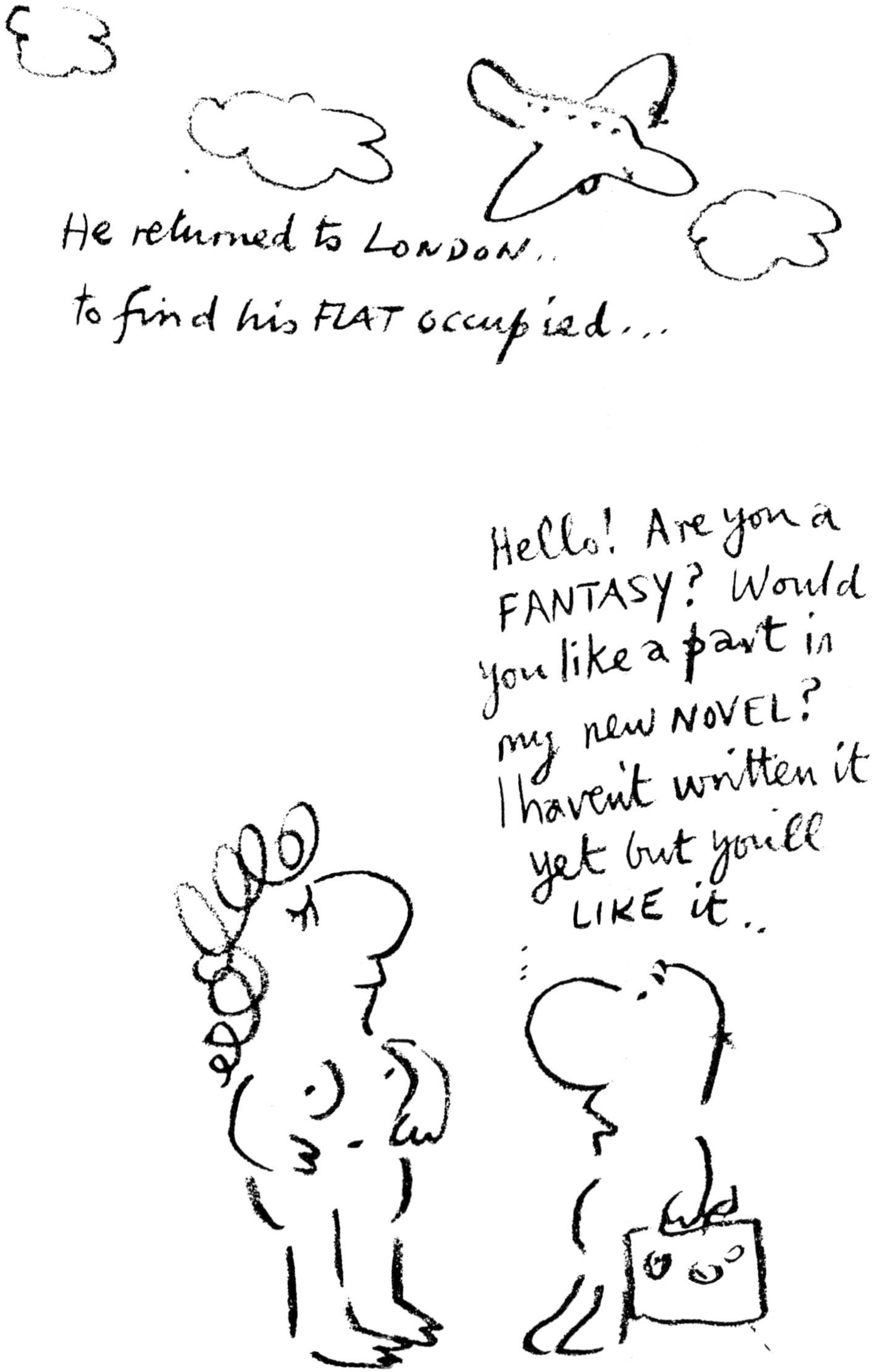
He returned to LONDON..
to find his FLAT occupied...
Hello! Are you a FANTASY? Would you like a part in my new NOVEL? I haven't written it yet but you'll LIKE it..

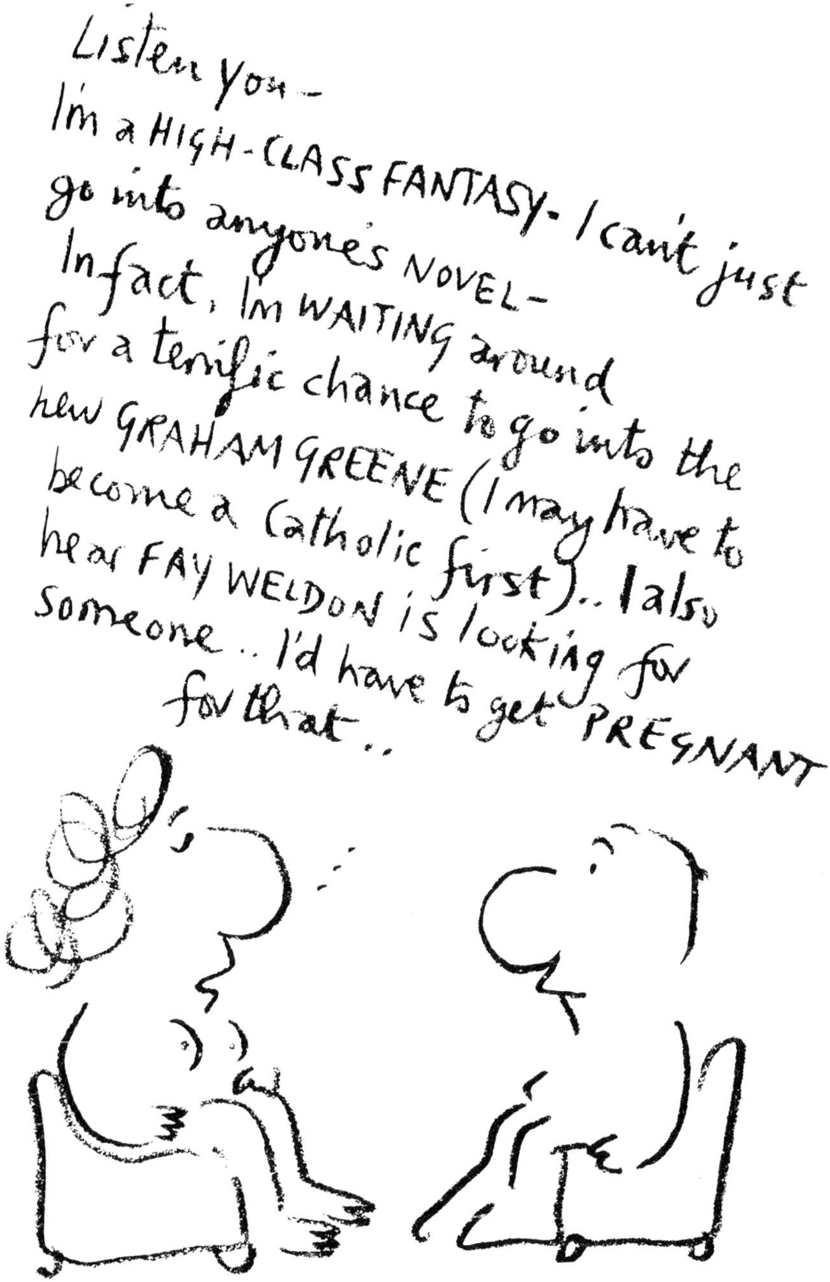
Listen you –
I'm a HIGH-CLASS FANTASY – I can't just
go into anyone's NOVEL –
In fact, I'm WAITING around
for a terrific chance to go into the
new GRAHAM GREENE (I may have to
become a Catholic first).. I also
hear FAY WELDON is looking for
someone.. I'd have to get PREGNANT
for that..

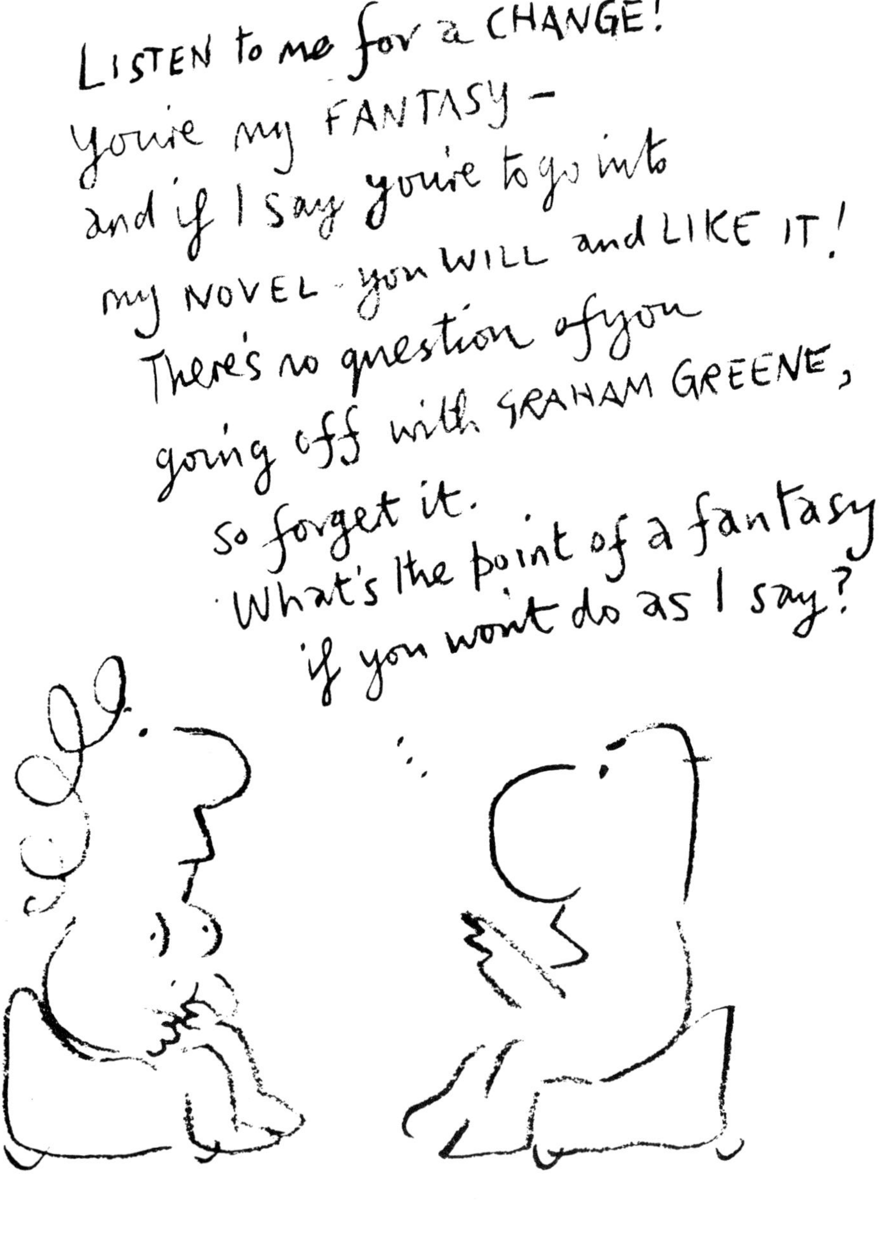
LISTEN to me for a CHANGE!
you're my FANTASY –
and if I say you're to go into
my NOVEL – you WILL and LIKE IT!
There's no question of you
going off with GRAHAM GREENE,
so forget it.
What's the point of a fantasy
if you won't do as I say?

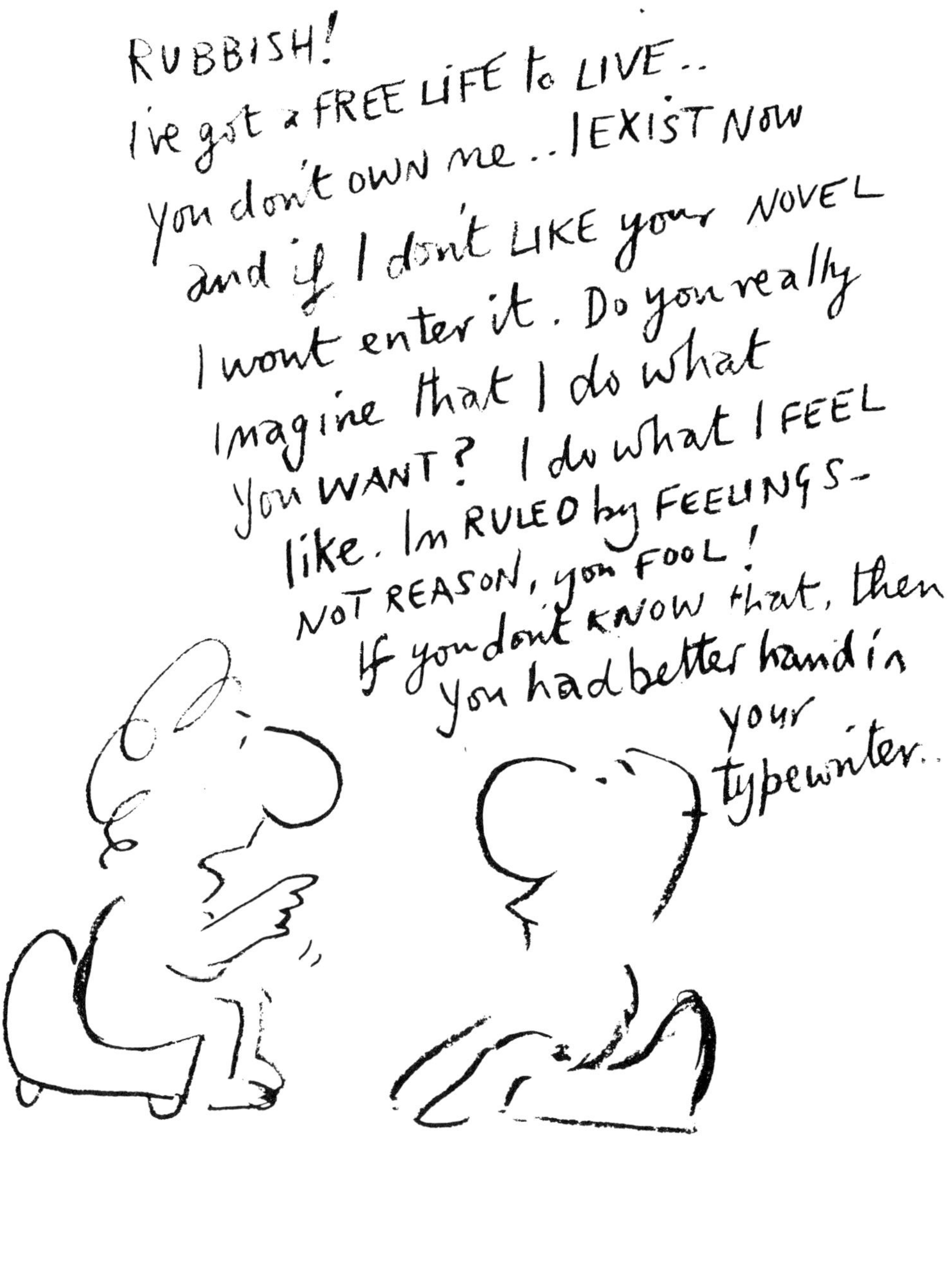
RUBBISH!
I've got a FREE LIFE to LIVE..
You don't OWN me.. I EXIST NOW
and if I don't LIKE your NOVEL
I won't enter it. Do you really
imagine that I do what
You WANT? I do what I FEEL
like. I'm RULED by FEELINGS -
NOT REASON, you FOOL!
If you don't KNOW that, then
You had better hand in
your
typewriter..

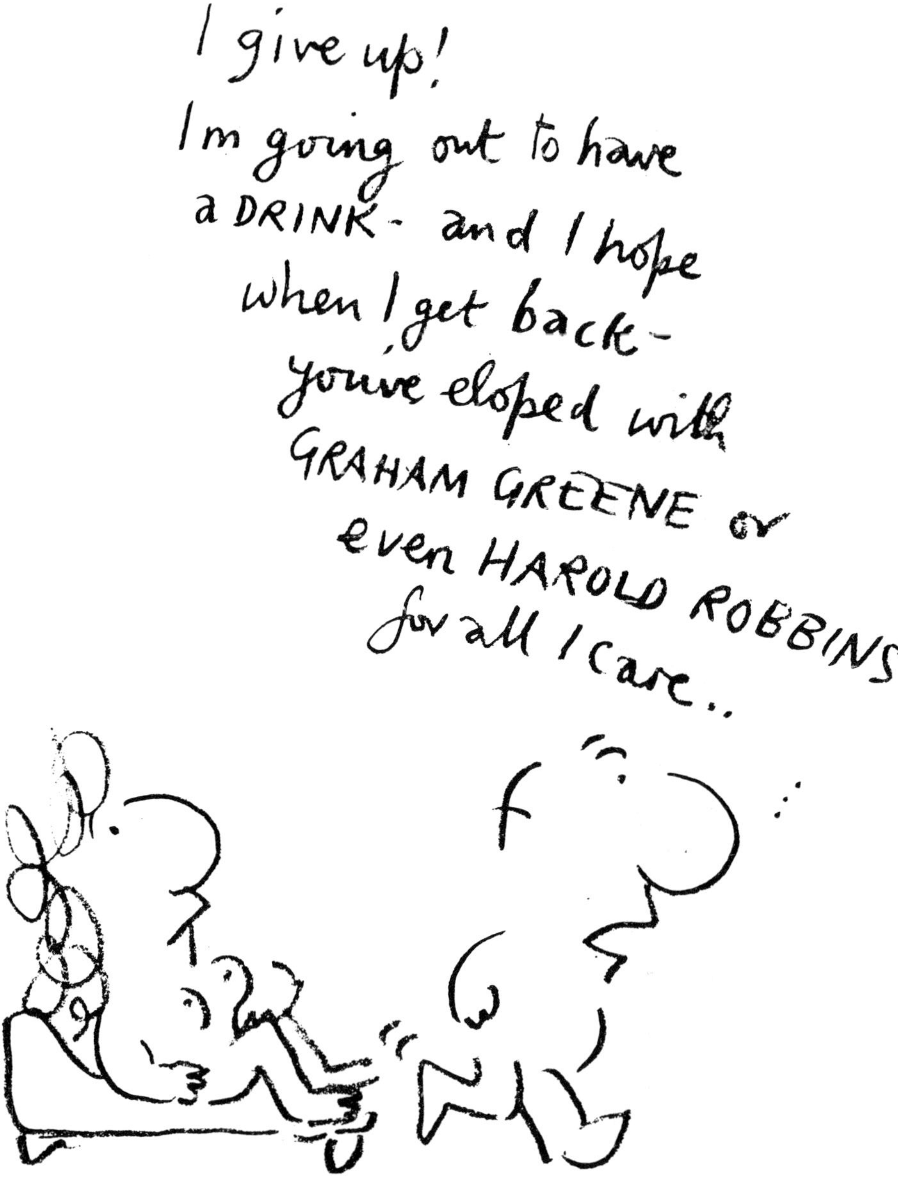
I give up!
I'm going out to have
a DRINK - and I hope
when I get back -
you've eloped with
GRAHAM GREENE or
even HAROLD ROBBINS
for all I care..

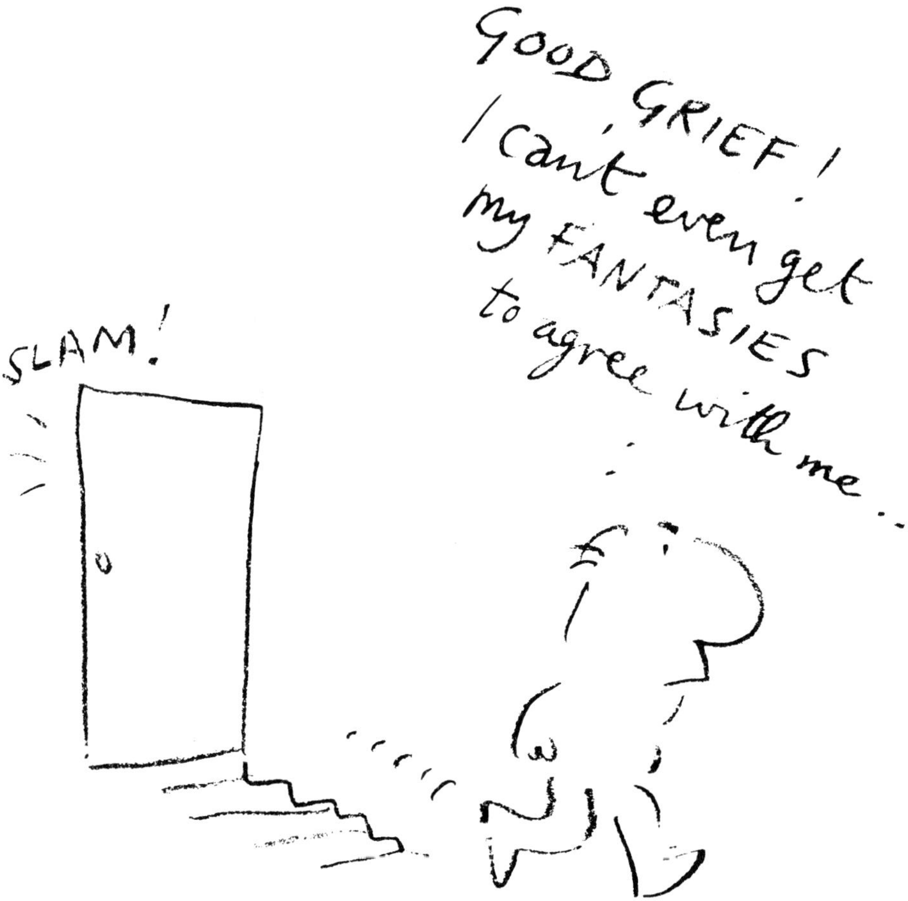
SLAM!
GOOD GRIEF! I can't even get my FANTASIES to agree with me...

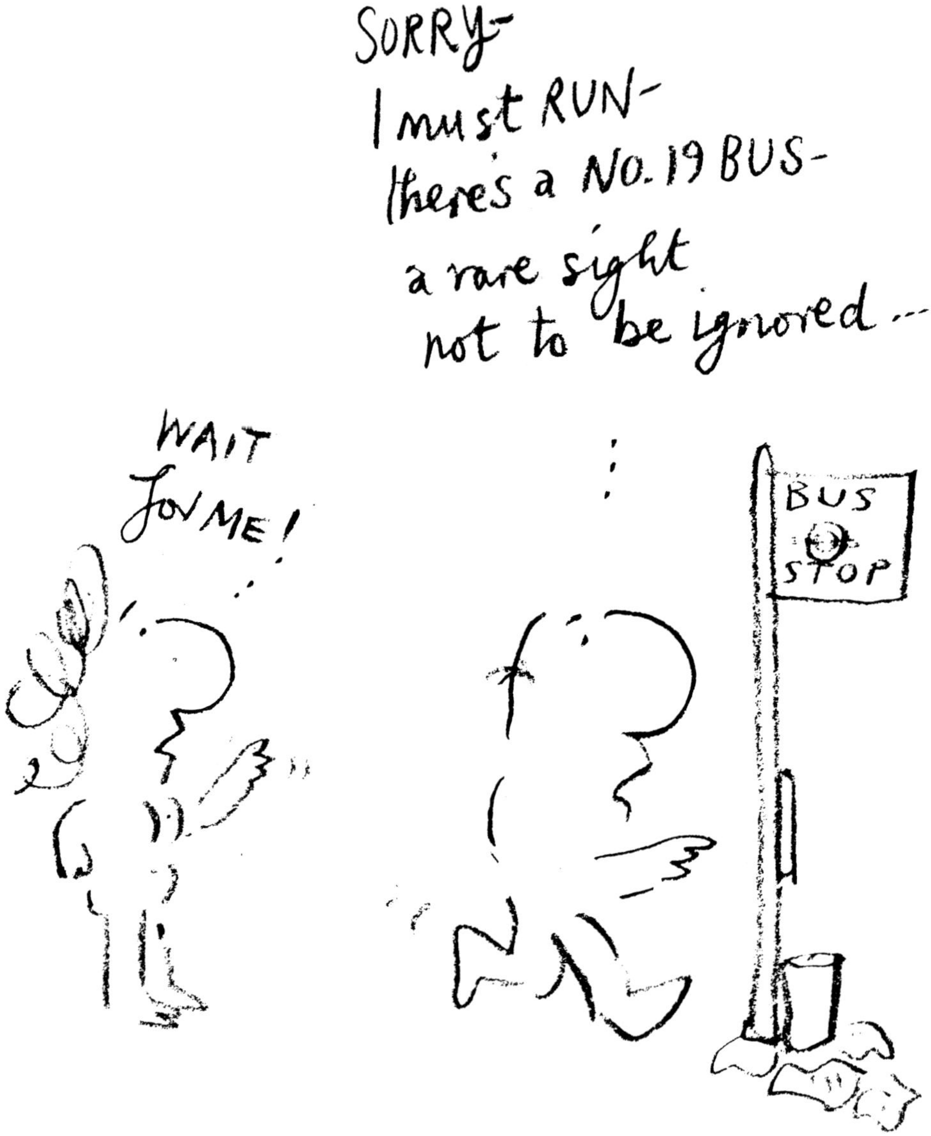
SORRY-
I must RUN-
there's a No. 19 BUS-
a rare sight
not to be ignored...
WAIT for ME!
BUS STOP

He sits quietly on the No 19 BUS —
trying to THINK quietly about
his NOVEL, the NATURE of ART
and LIFE, TOLSTOY, DOSTOIEVSKY,
DICKENS and why BUS FARES
have gone up again..

The CONDUCTOR turns to speak to him ...

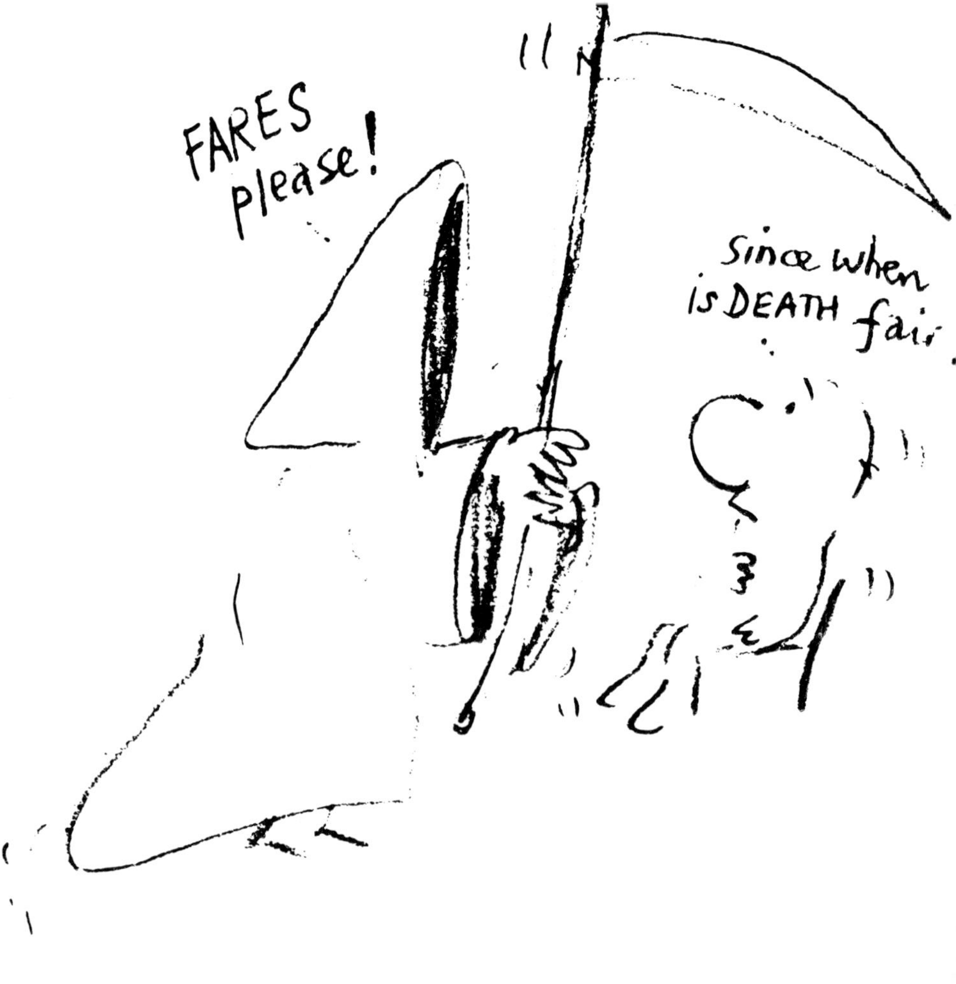
FARES please!
Since when is DEATH fair

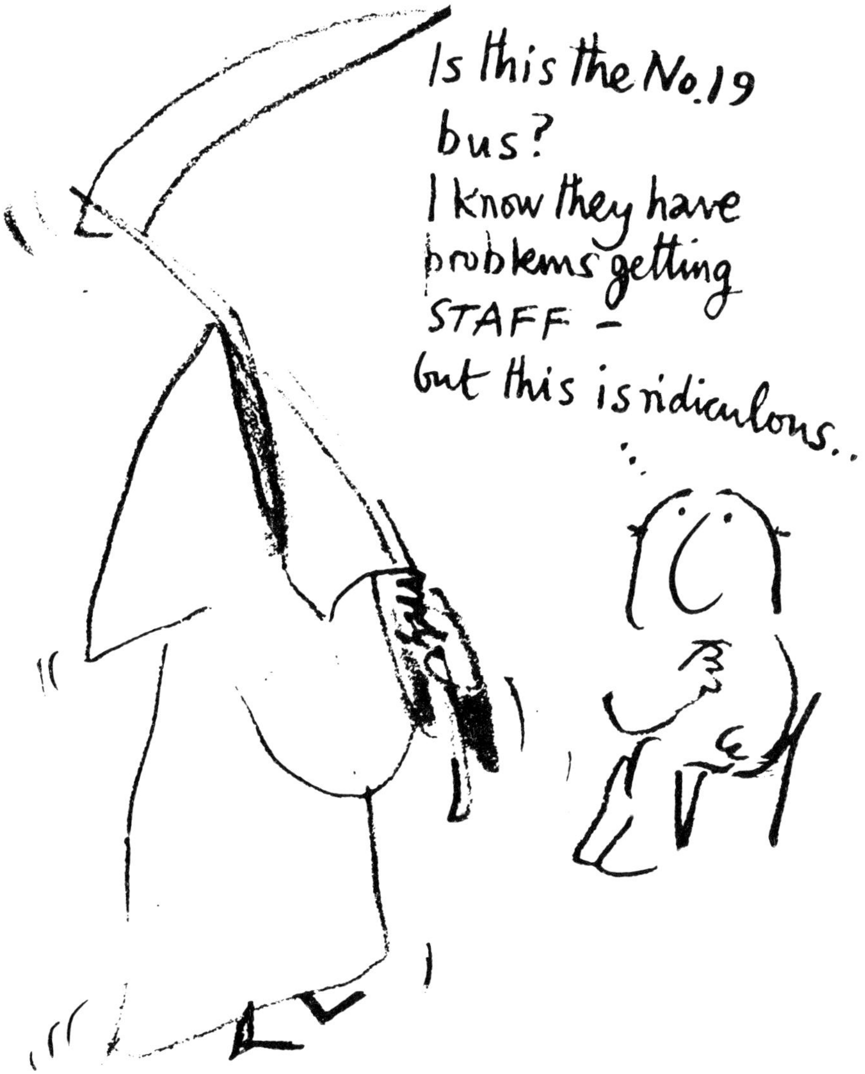
Is this the No.19 bus?
I know they have problems getting STAFF –
but this is ridiculous...

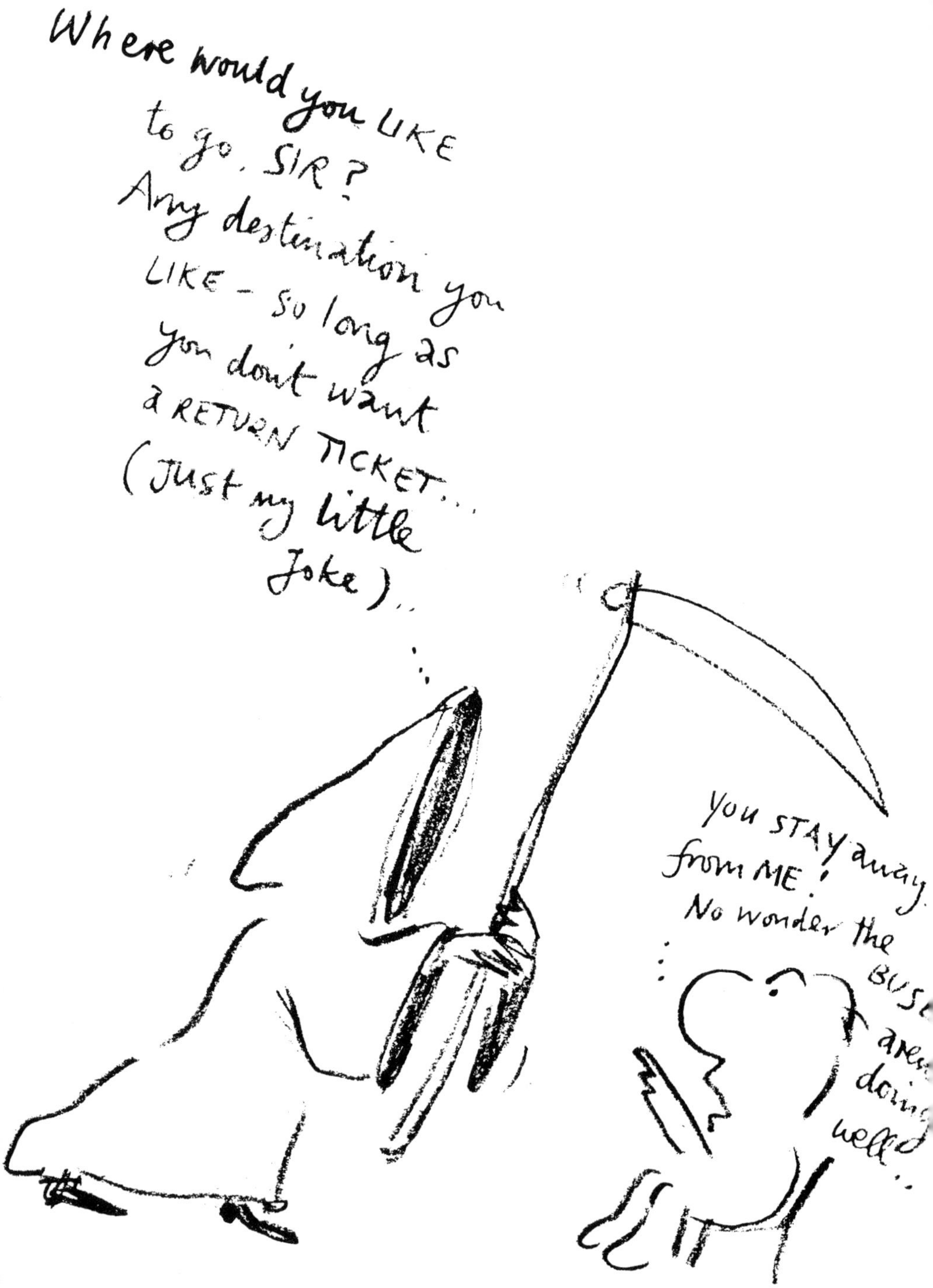
Where would you LIKE to go, SIR? Any destination you LIKE – so long as you don't want a RETURN TICKET... (JUST my little Joke)...
YOU STAY away from ME! No wonder the BUSES are doing well!...

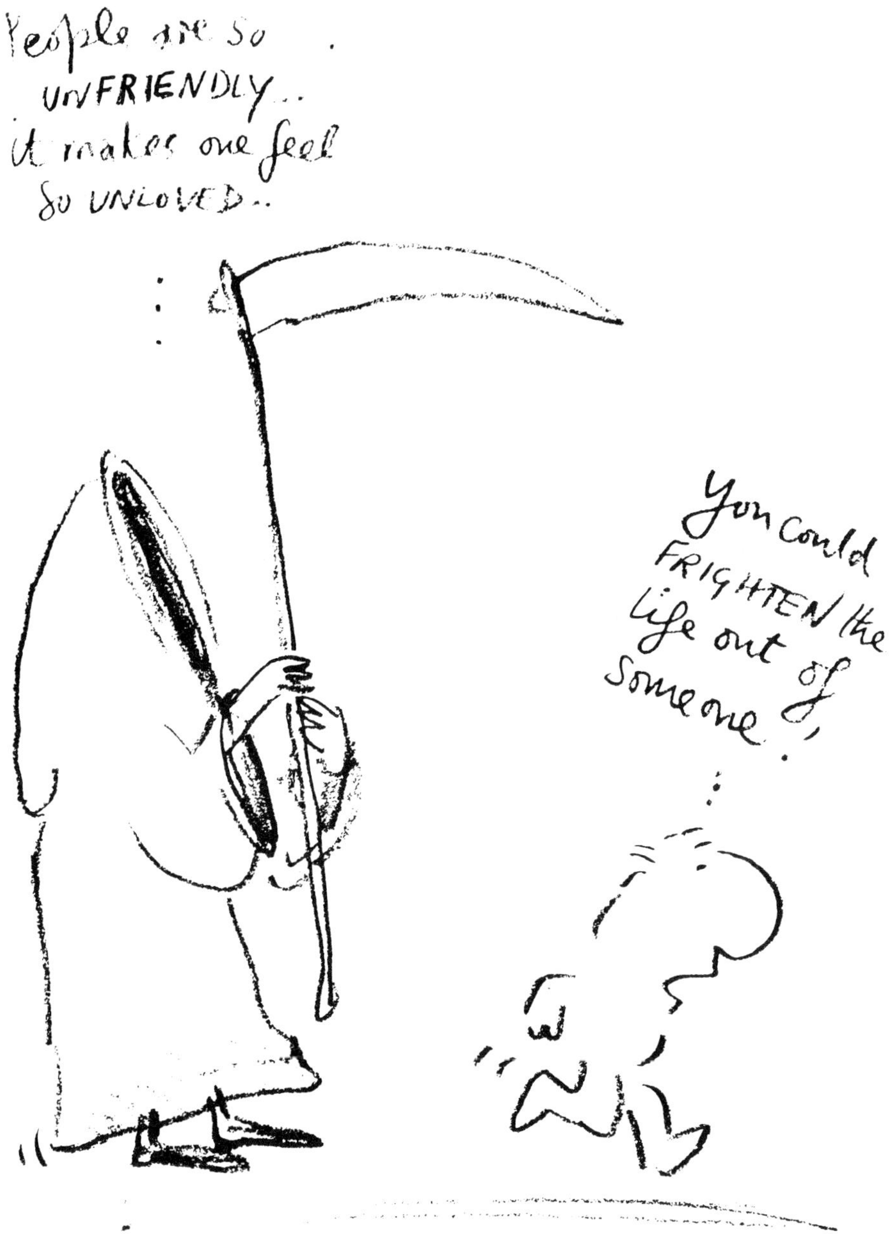
People are so UNFRIENDLY... it makes one feel so UNLOVED..
You could FRIGHTEN the life out of someone!

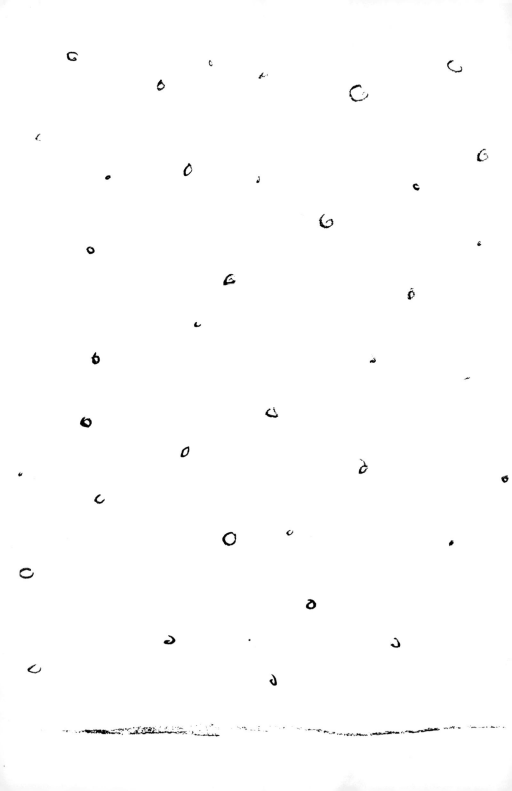

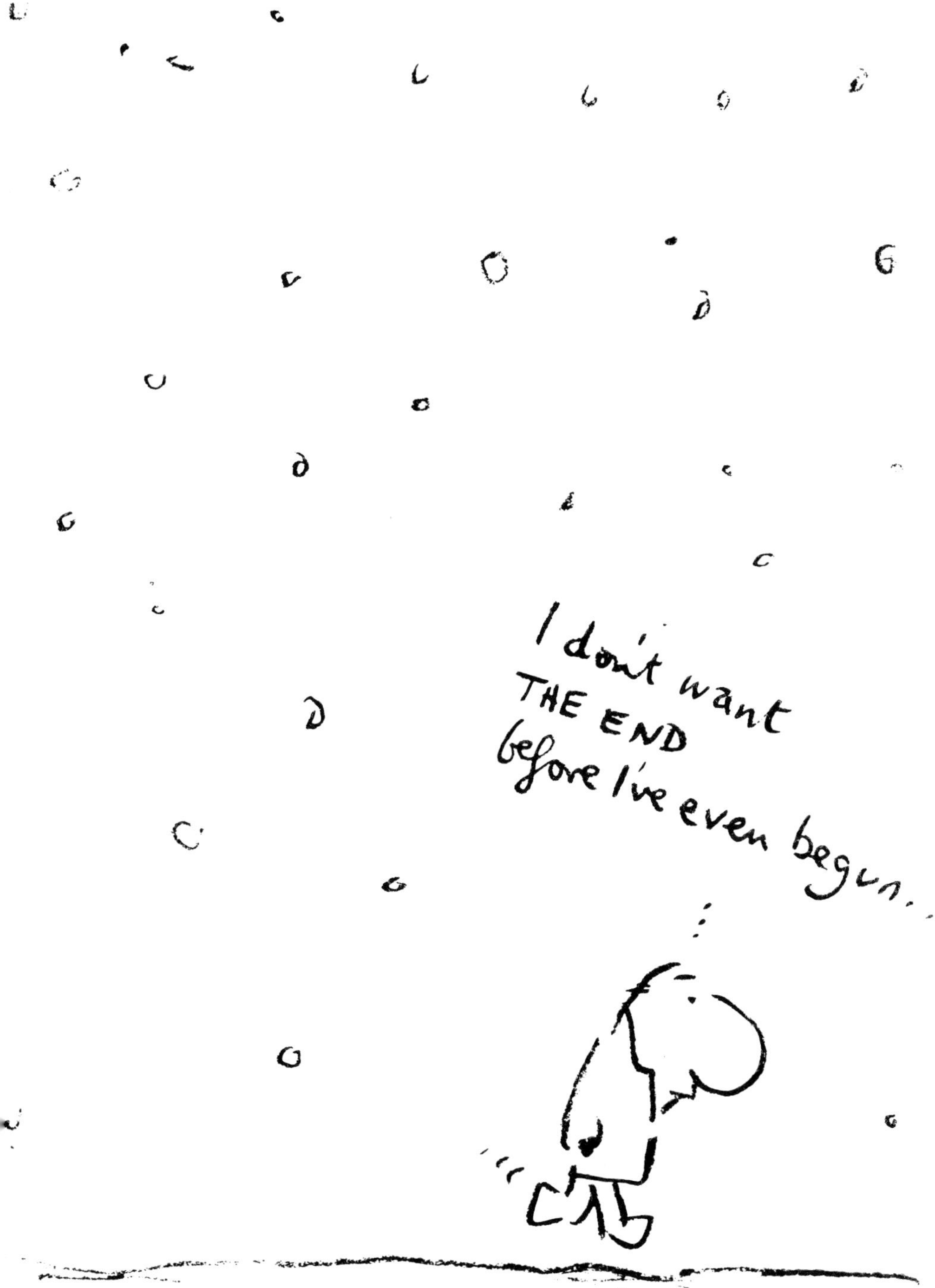
I don't want
THE END
before I've even begun...

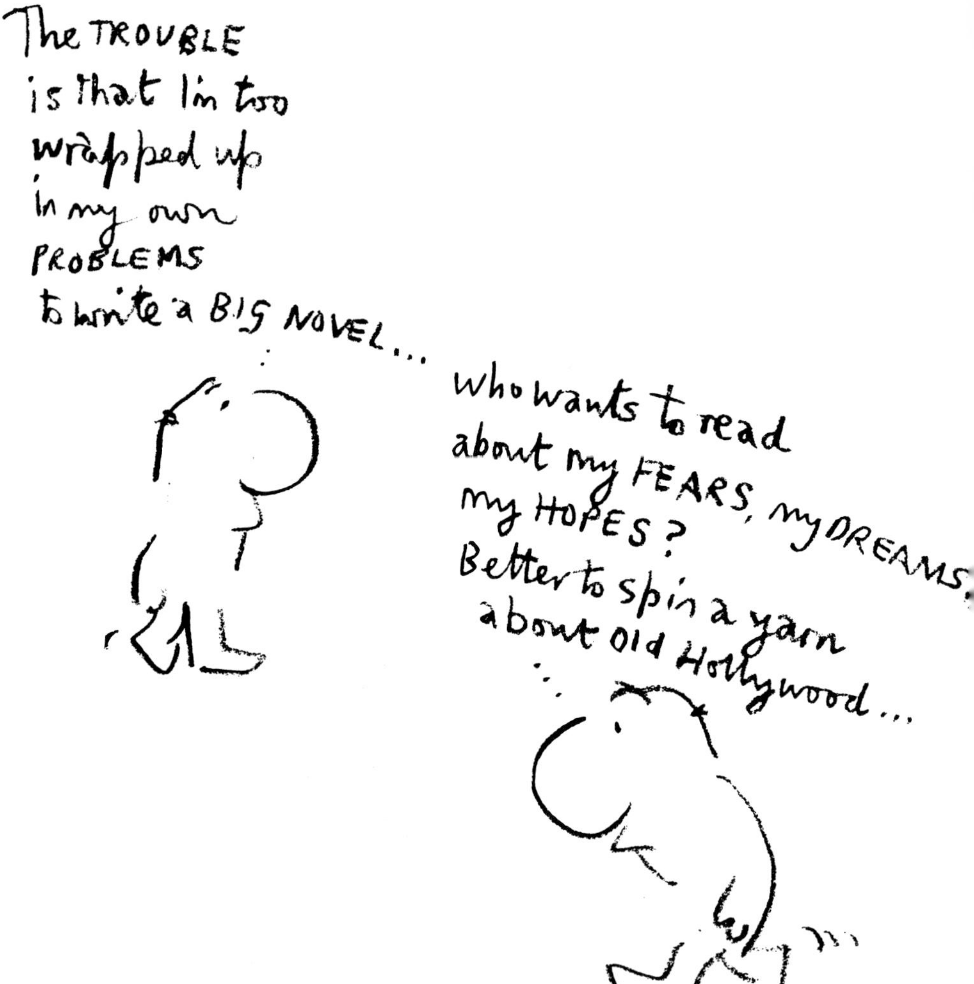
The TROUBLE
is that I'm too
wrapped up
in my own
PROBLEMS
to write a BIG NOVEL...
who wants to read
about my FEARS, my DREAMS,
my HOPES?
Better to spin a yarn
about old Hollywood...

and
Sexual encounters of
a Deviant Kind .. of COKE-
SNORTING beside LAKE-SIZED
POOLS..
But I don't know HOLLYWOOD –

All I know
is my own LIFE..

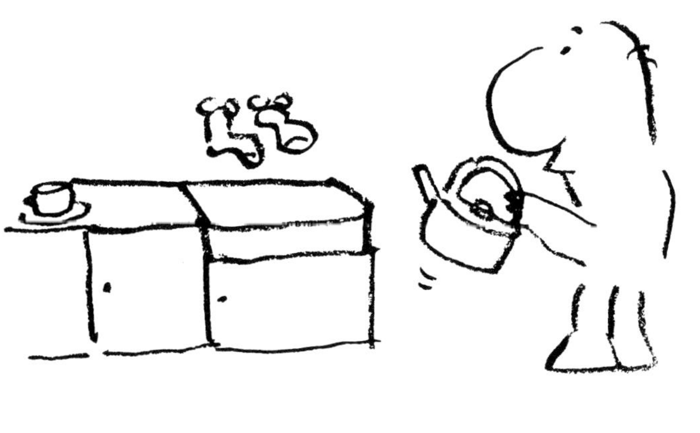

Which is very BORING –
it's cups of TEA and listening to the RADIO
and walking to the BAKERS to
buy two TEACAKES and a SMALL
Wholemeal LOAF.. and cooking
a LAMB CHOP for supper..
(I want to leave quietly without PAIN and
with a burst of MOZART in my ears..)

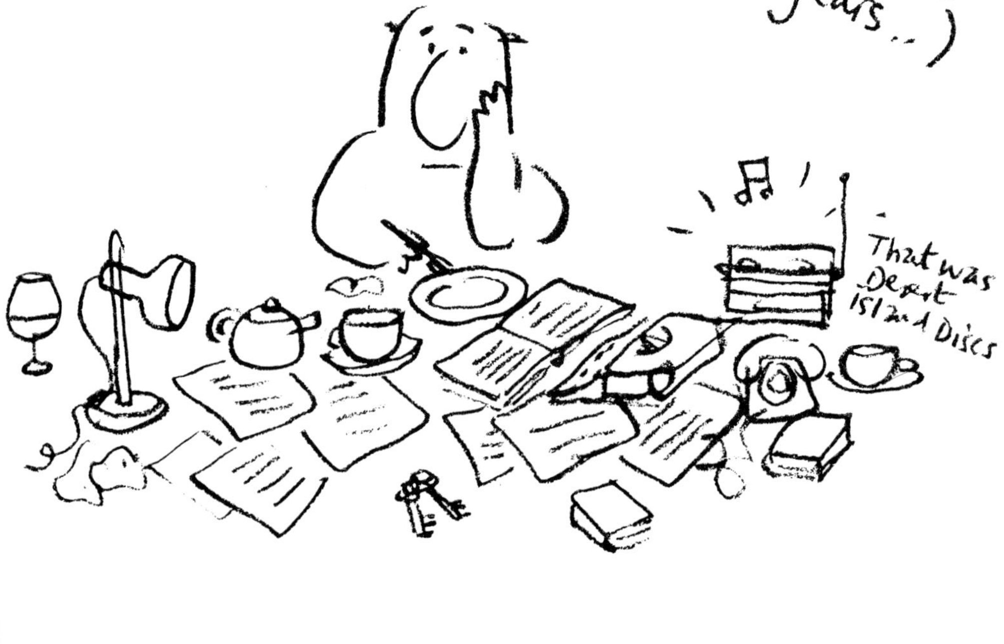
That was Desert Island Discs

Which reminds me –
I must go out and BUY a loaf of
BREAD. The BAKER closes
at 4 o'clock (Why?) It's only 3.30
and I feel TIRED.. Perhaps
I should have a NAP now and
wake up nice and fresh later...
THE NOVEL will still be
there .. LIFE needs BREAD..
and LIFE must come before
ART – and a SNOOZE
comes even before
BREAD itself..

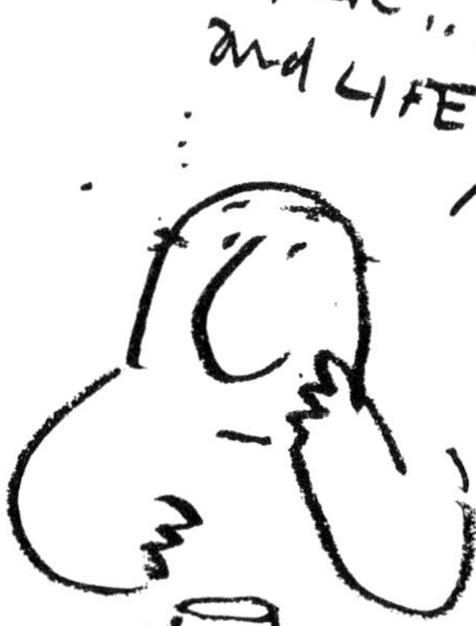

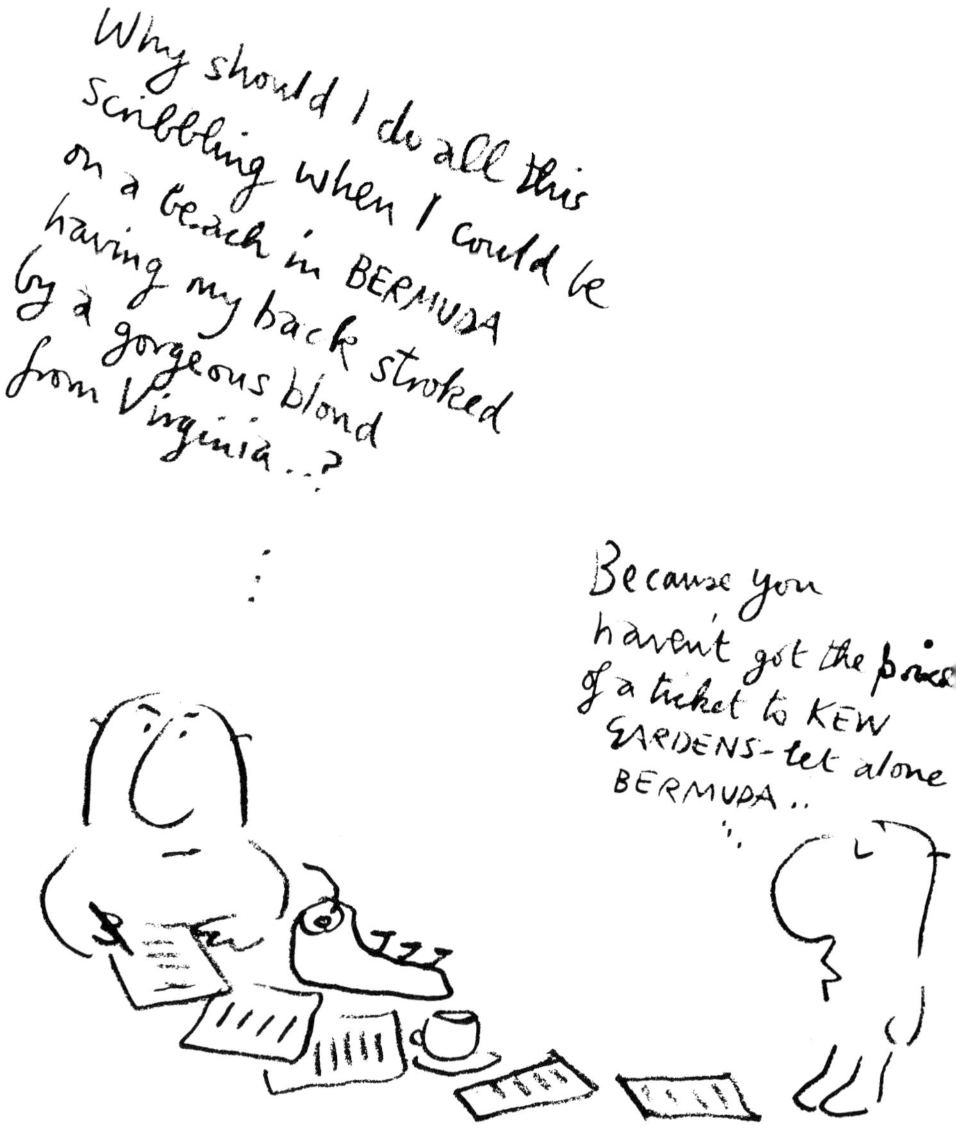
Why should I do all this scribbling when I could be on a beach in BERMUDA having my back stroked by a gorgeous blond from Virginia ..?
Because you haven't got the price of a ticket to KEW GARDENS - let alone BERMUDA ..

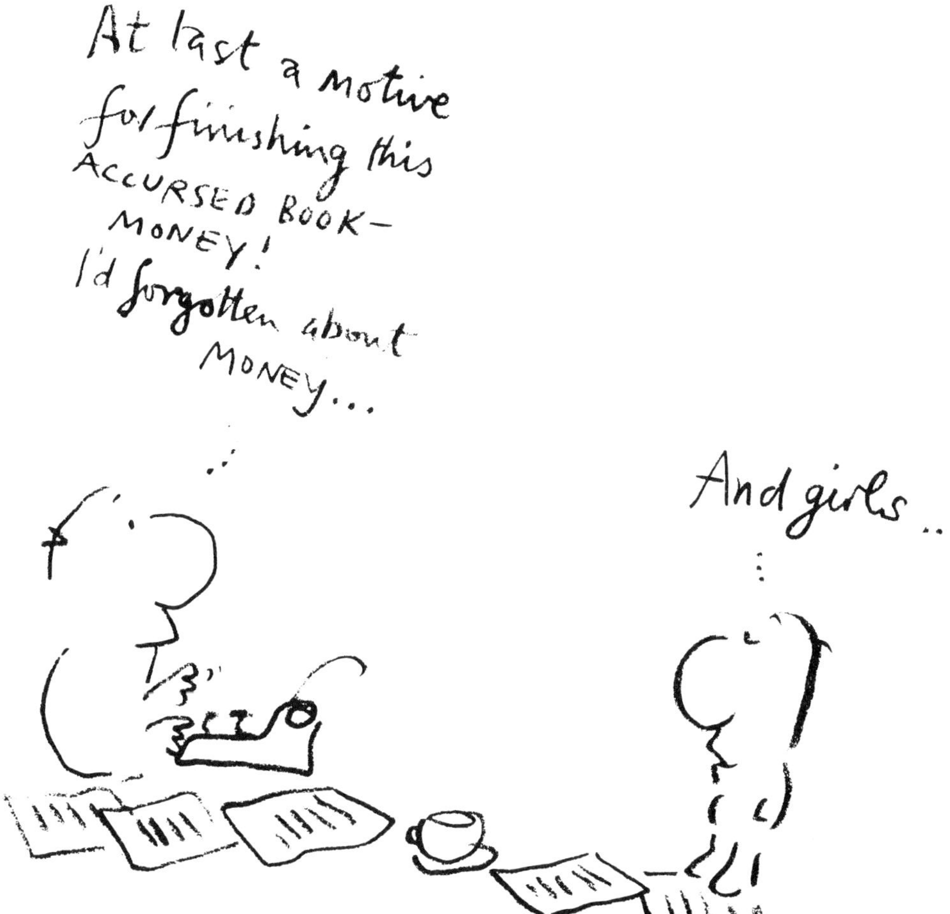
At last a motive for finishing this ACCURSED BOOK- MONEY! I'd forgotten about MONEY...
And girls..

GIRLS!
GIRLS!
Is that all you think about?
No - I sometimes think about SEX..
GIRLS

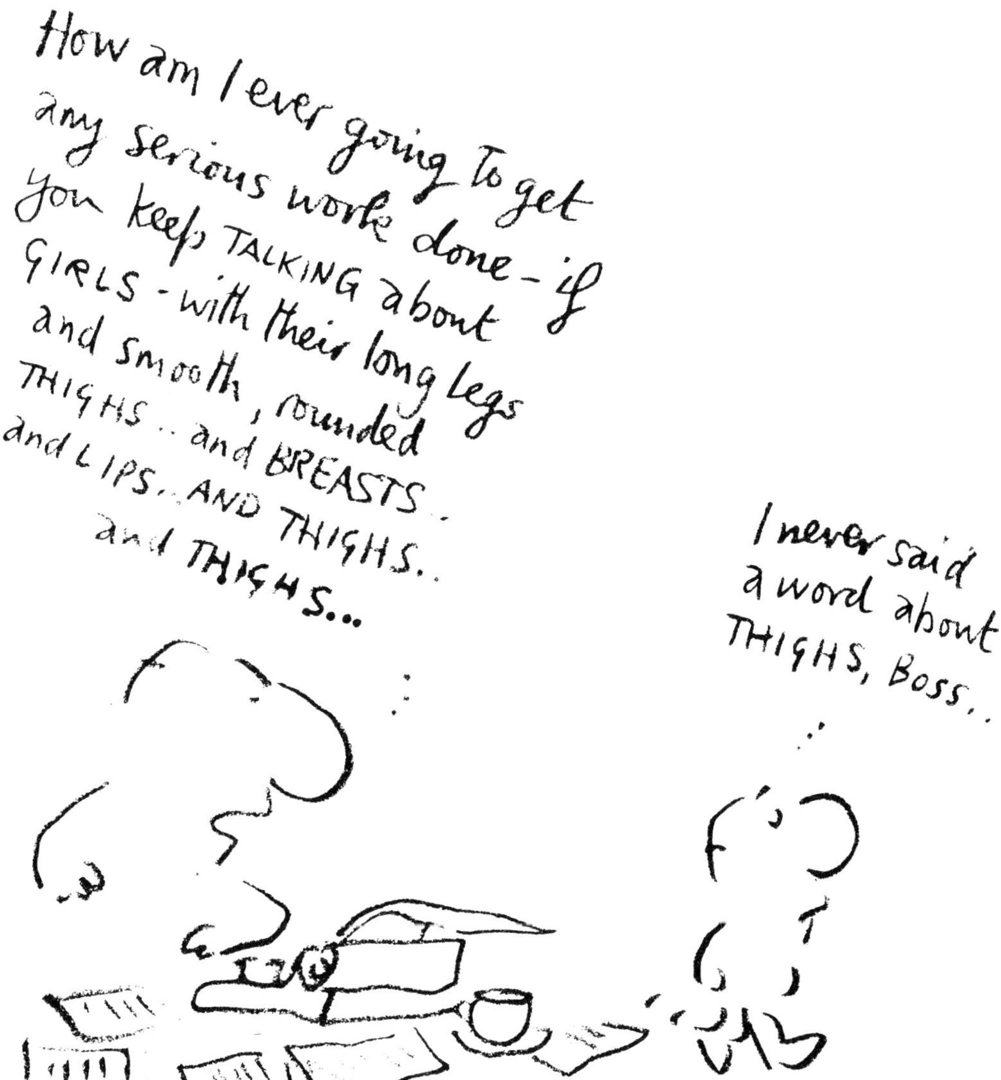
How am I ever going to get any serious work done - if you keep TALKING about GIRLS - with their long legs and smooth, rounded THIGHS .. and BREASTS .. and LIPS .. AND THIGHS .. and THIGHS...
I never said a word about THIGHS, Boss..

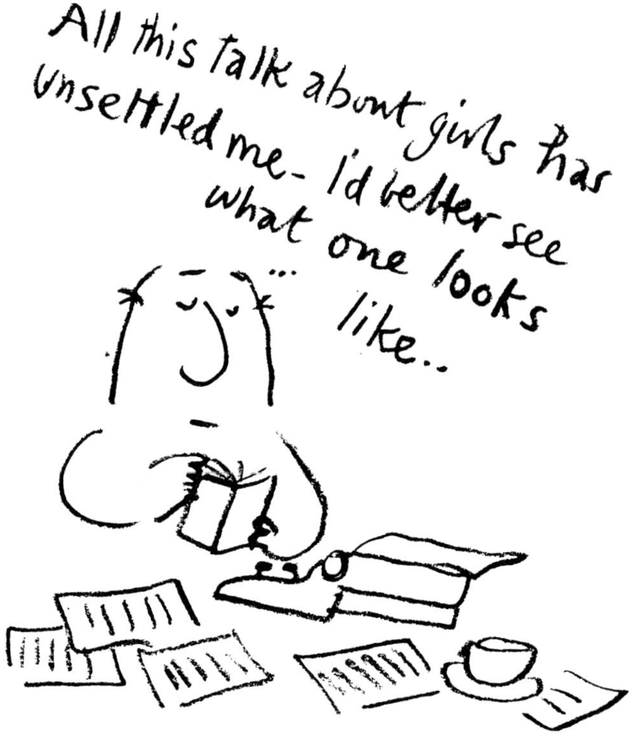
All this talk about girls has unsettled me - I'd better see what one looks like...

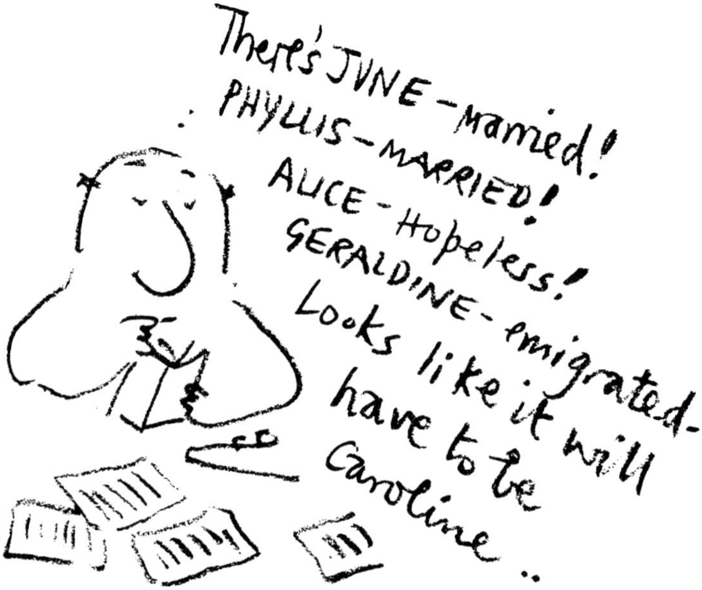
There's JUNE - married!
PHYLLIS - MARRIED!
ALICE - Hopeless!
GERALDINE - emigrated -
Looks like it will have to be Caroline..

The next evening at a SMART RESTAURANT in MAYFAIR .. where FAMOUS NAMES eat...

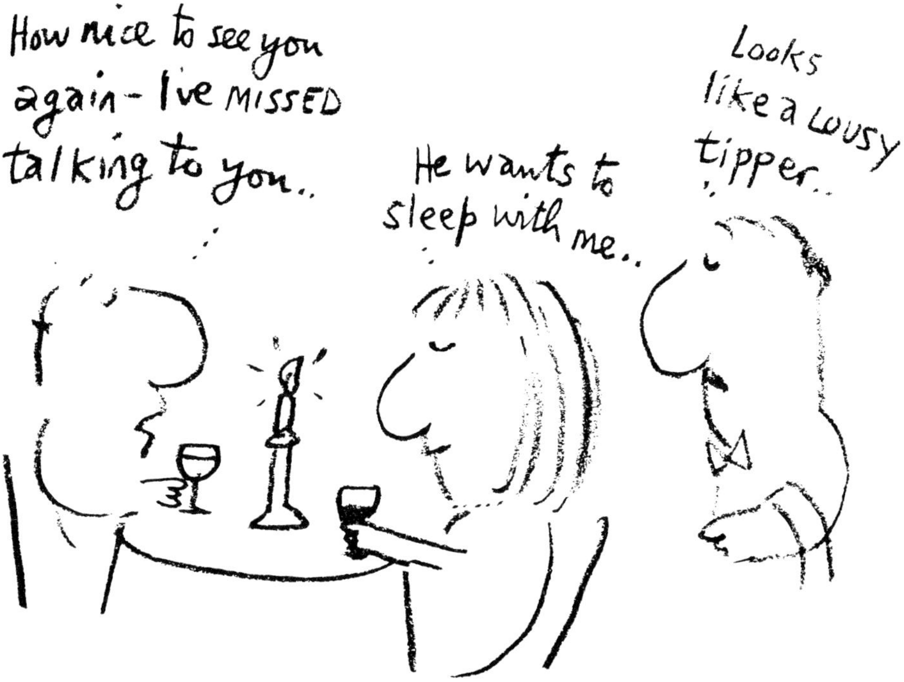
How nice to see you again - I've MISSED talking to you..
He wants to sleep with me..
Looks like a LOUSY tipper..

Didn't that man used to be STEWART GRANGER?
You can have anything you LIKE – So long as it's NOT in a HURRY..
Excuse Me, SIR – but I think you dropped this NAME..
JOAN COLLINS
Isn't that MICHAEL CAINE? Some more vino? It suits you to DRINK.. I mean I Love talking to you – your MIND is so.. so..
He BADLY wants to sleep with me
I wish I could remember her name – used to be Married to someone..

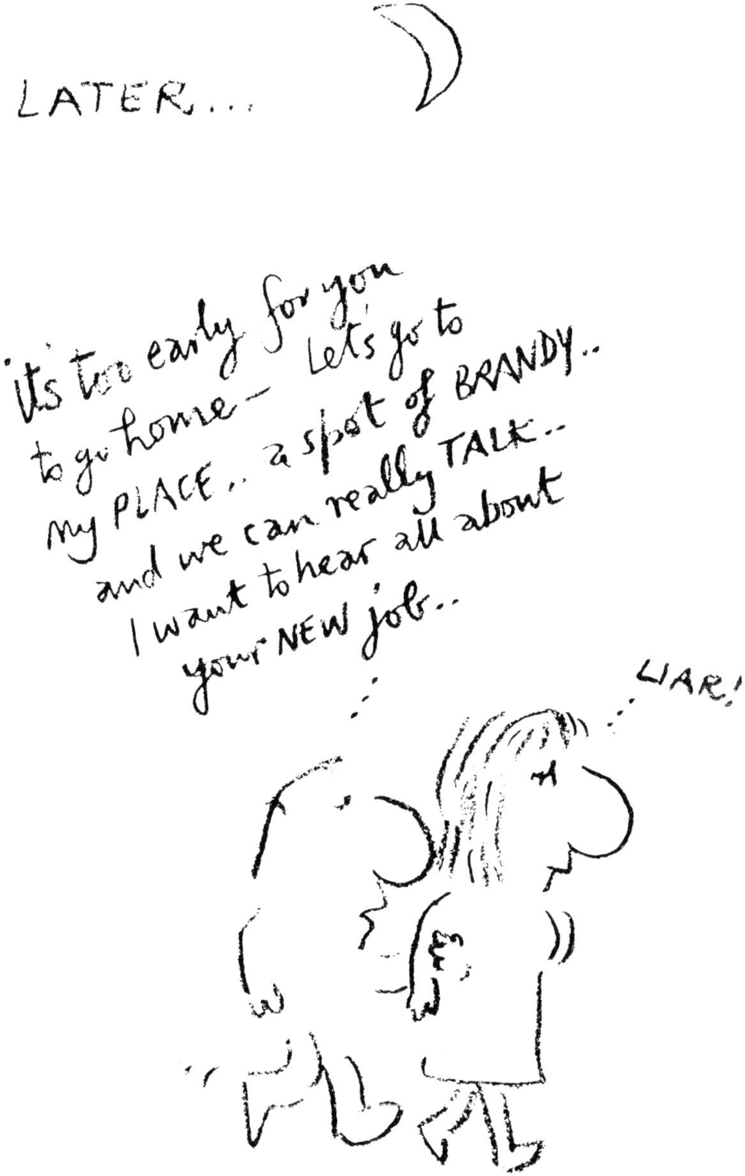
LATER...
it's too early for you to go home — Let's go to my PLACE.. a spot of BRANDY.. and we can really TALK.. I want to hear all about your NEW job..
...LIAR!

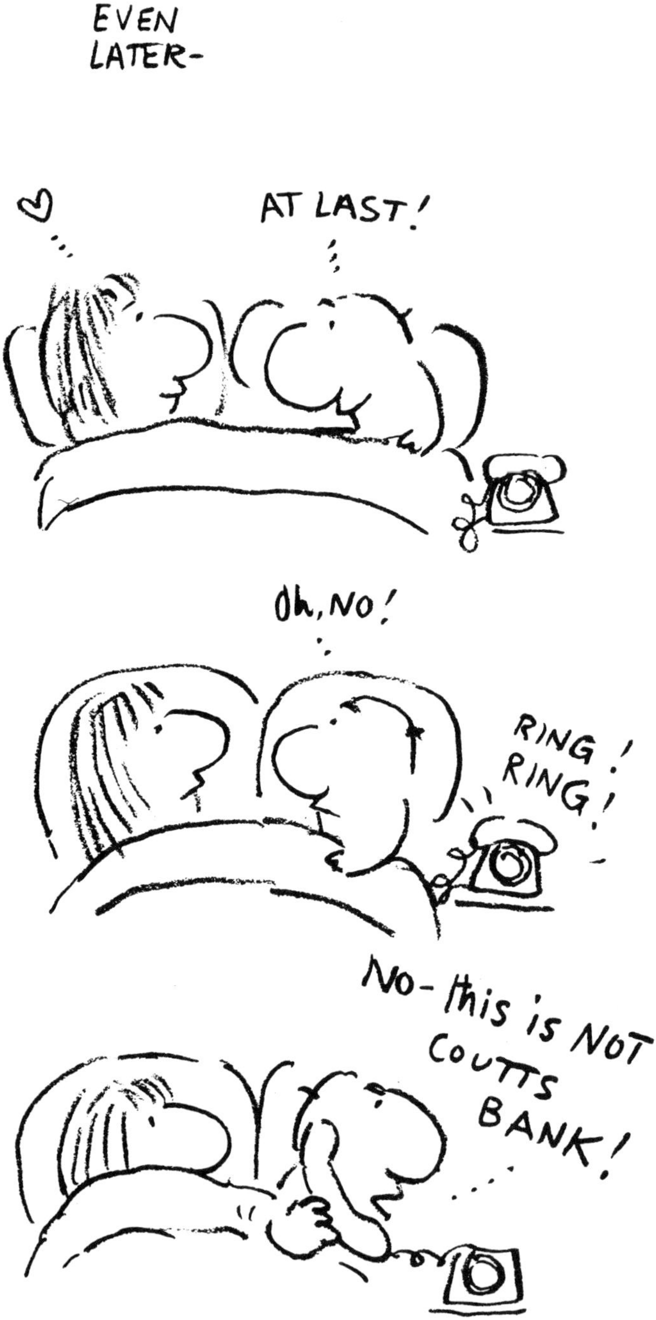
EVEN LATER-
AT LAST!
Oh, NO!
RING! RING!
No- this is NOT COUTTS BANK!

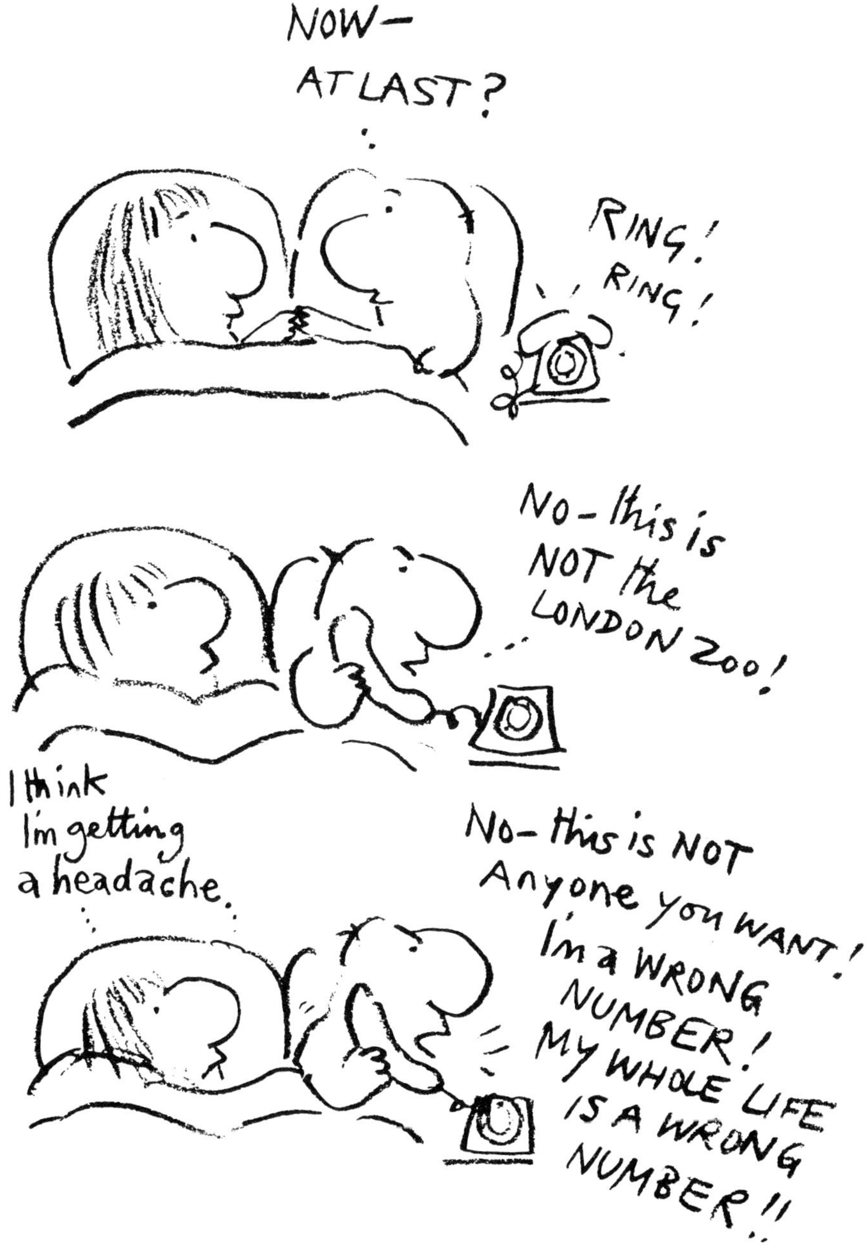
NOW-
AT LAST?
RING! RING!
No- this is NOT the LONDON ZOO!
I think I'm getting a headache..
No- this is NOT Anyone you WANT! I'm a WRONG NUMBER! My WHOLE LIFE IS A WRONG NUMBER!!

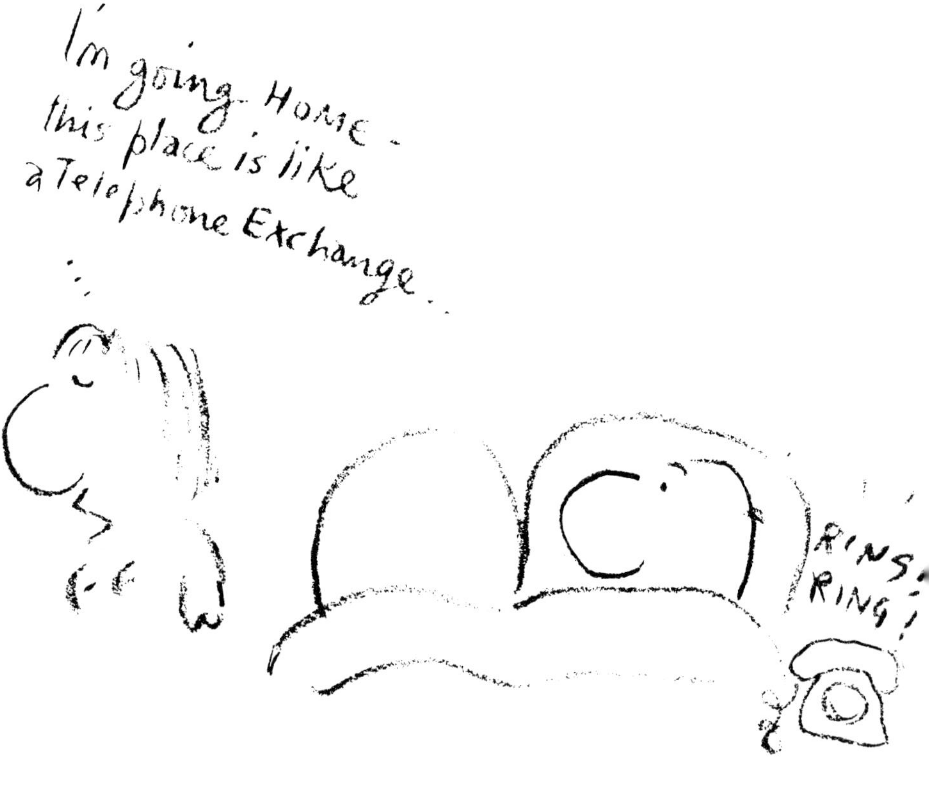
I'm going HOME - this place is like a Telephone Exchange...
RING, RING!

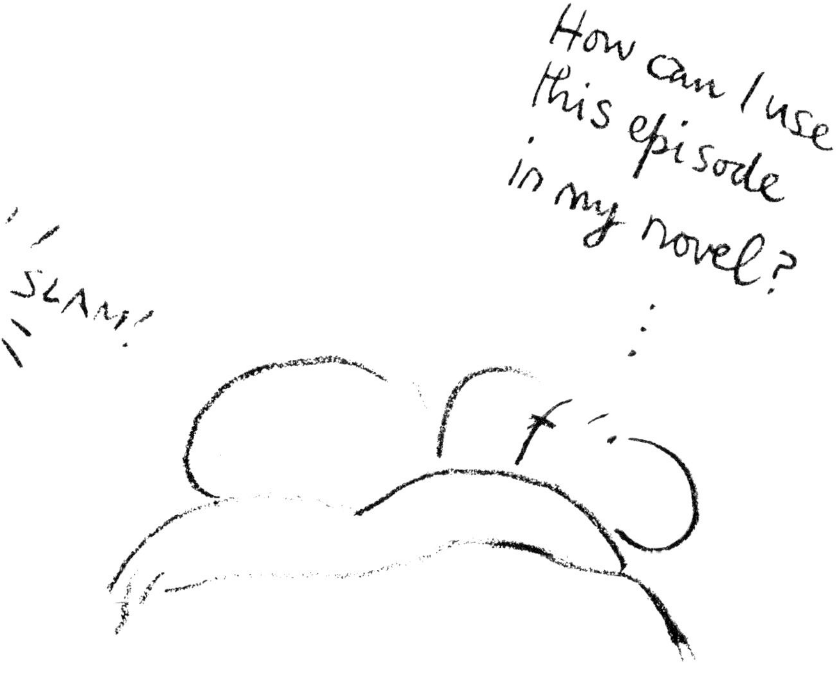
How can I use this episode in my novel?
SLAM!

The NEXT DAY...

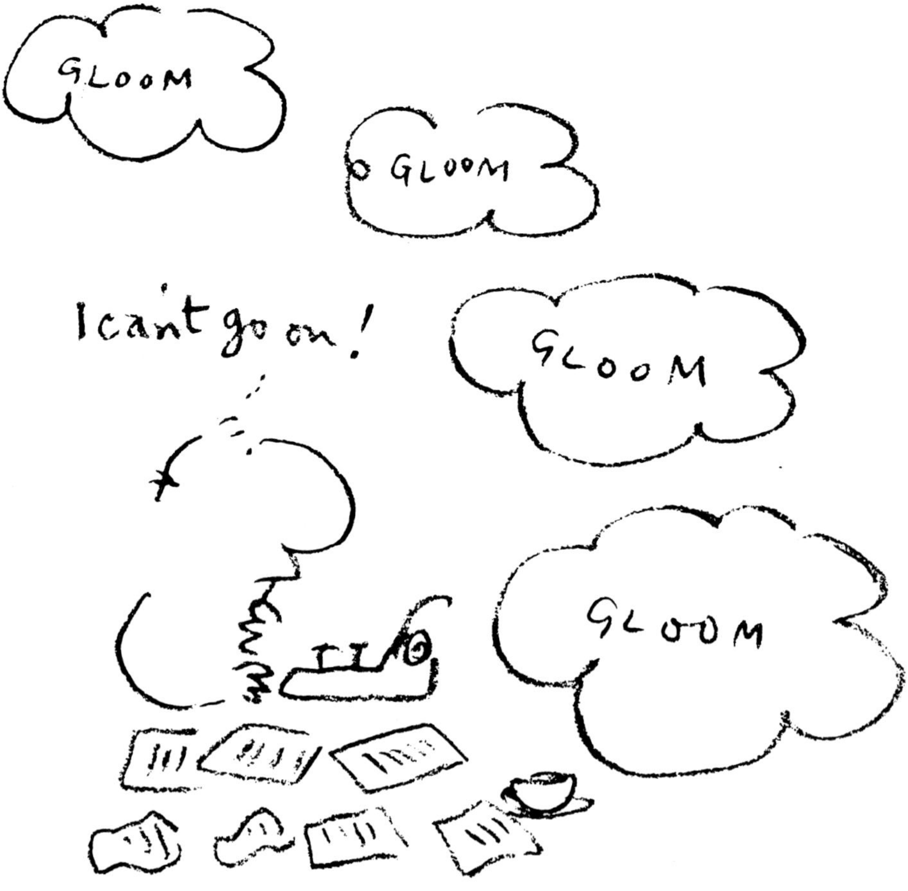
GLOOM
GLOOM
I can't go on!
GLOOM
GLOOM

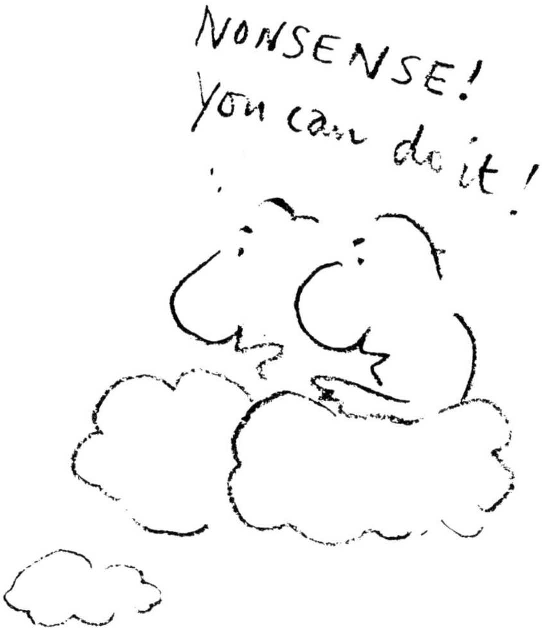
NONSENSE!
You can do it!

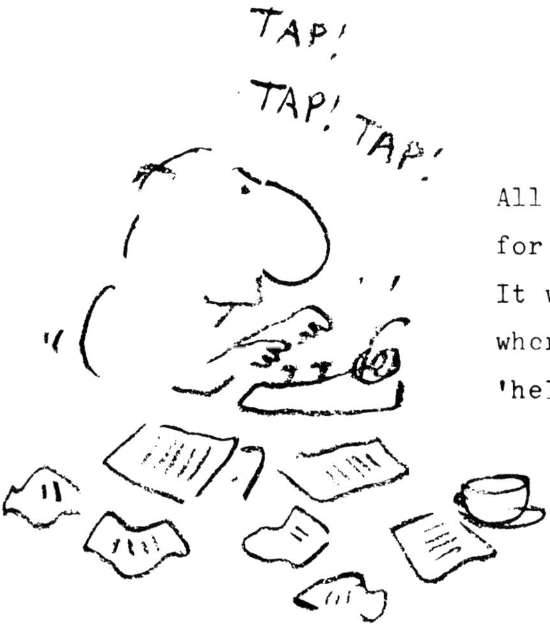
TAP!
TAP! TAP!

Chapter One

All that summer he yearned for sex...

It was one of those parties where people kept saying 'hello' and

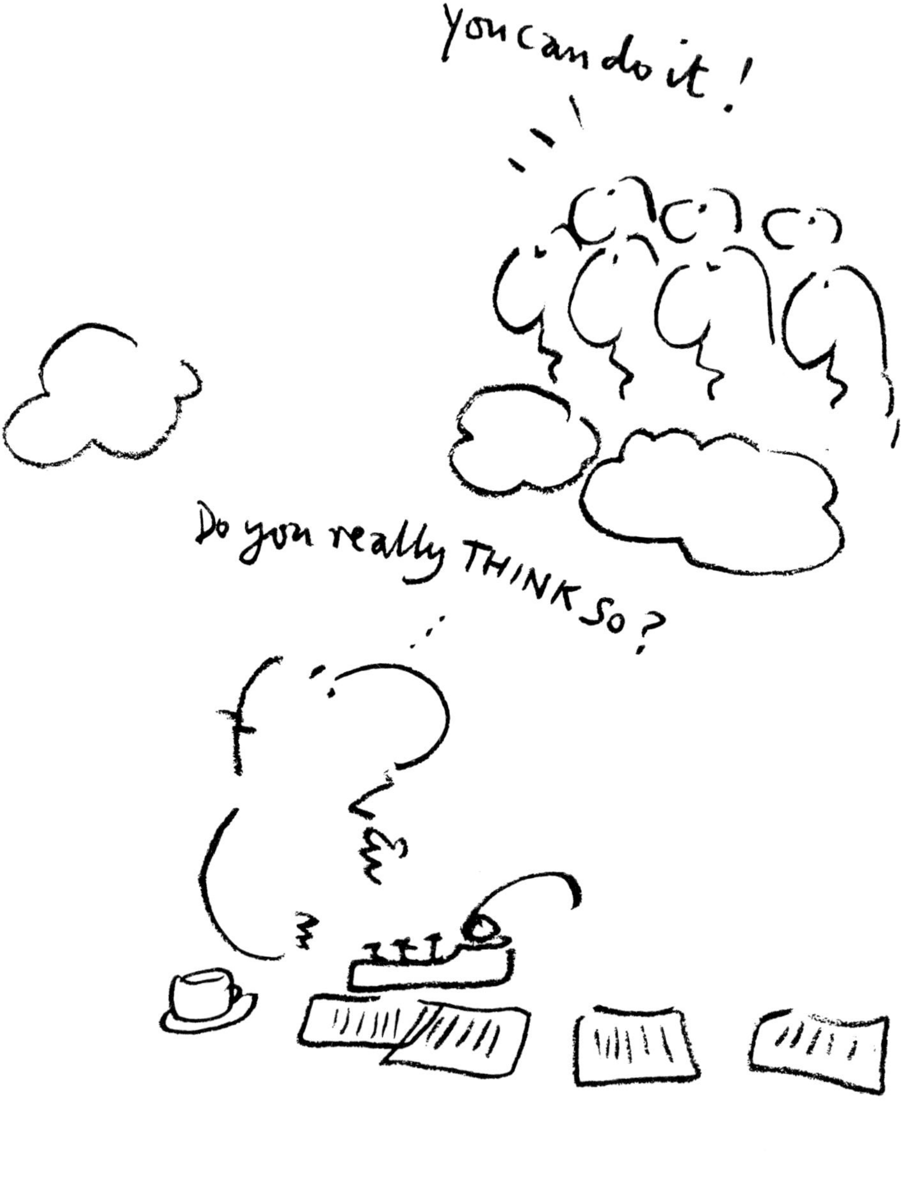
You can do it!
Do you really THINK so?

you can do it!
THINK of the FOYLES LITERARY LUNCH!
The BOOKER PRIZE!!
JUST GO FORWARD!

ALL TOGETHER NOW!

GO FORWARD...

one page...at a time...

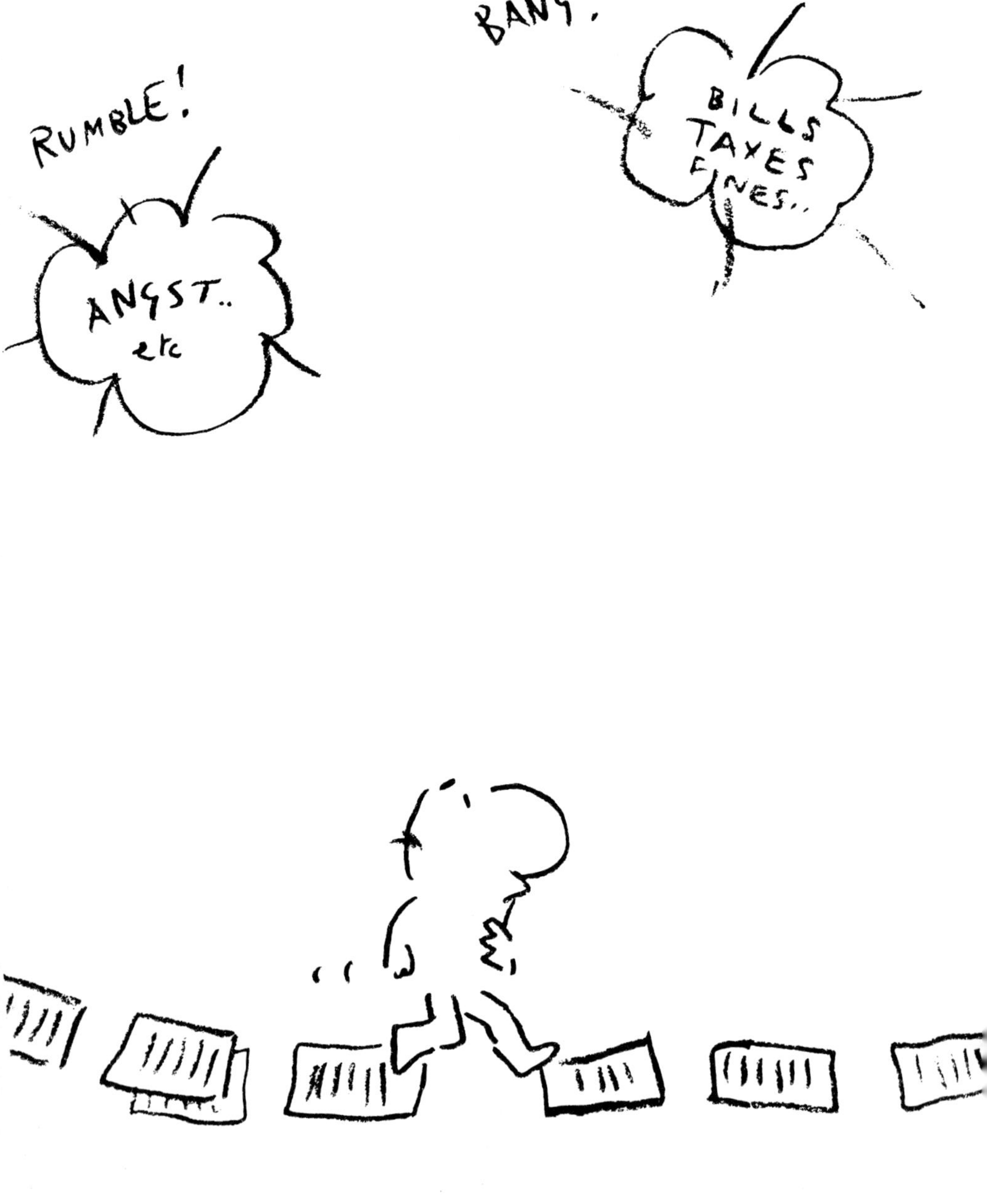

RUMBLE!
ANGST..
etc
BANG!
BILLS
TAXES
FINES..

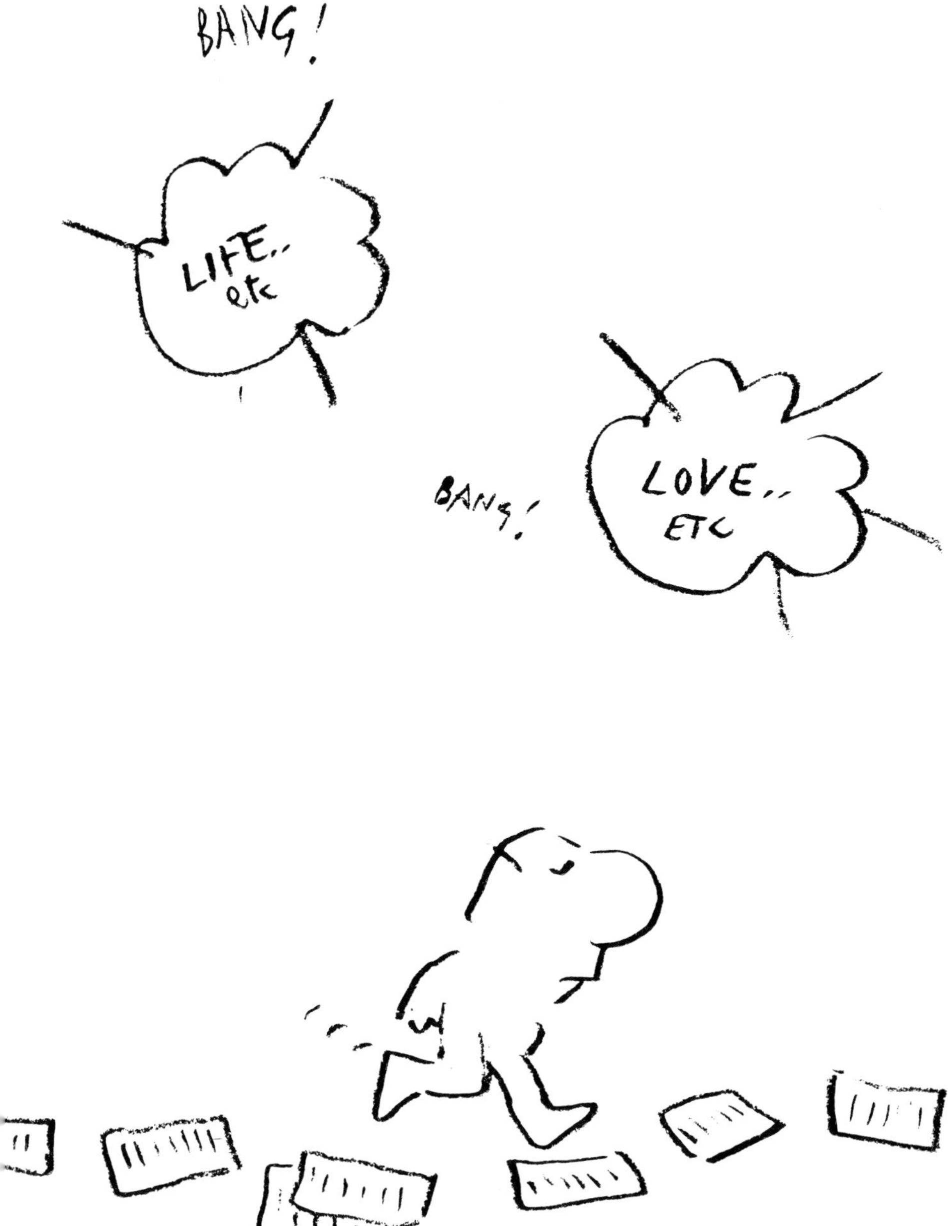
BANG!
LIFE..
etc
BANG!
LOVE..
ETC

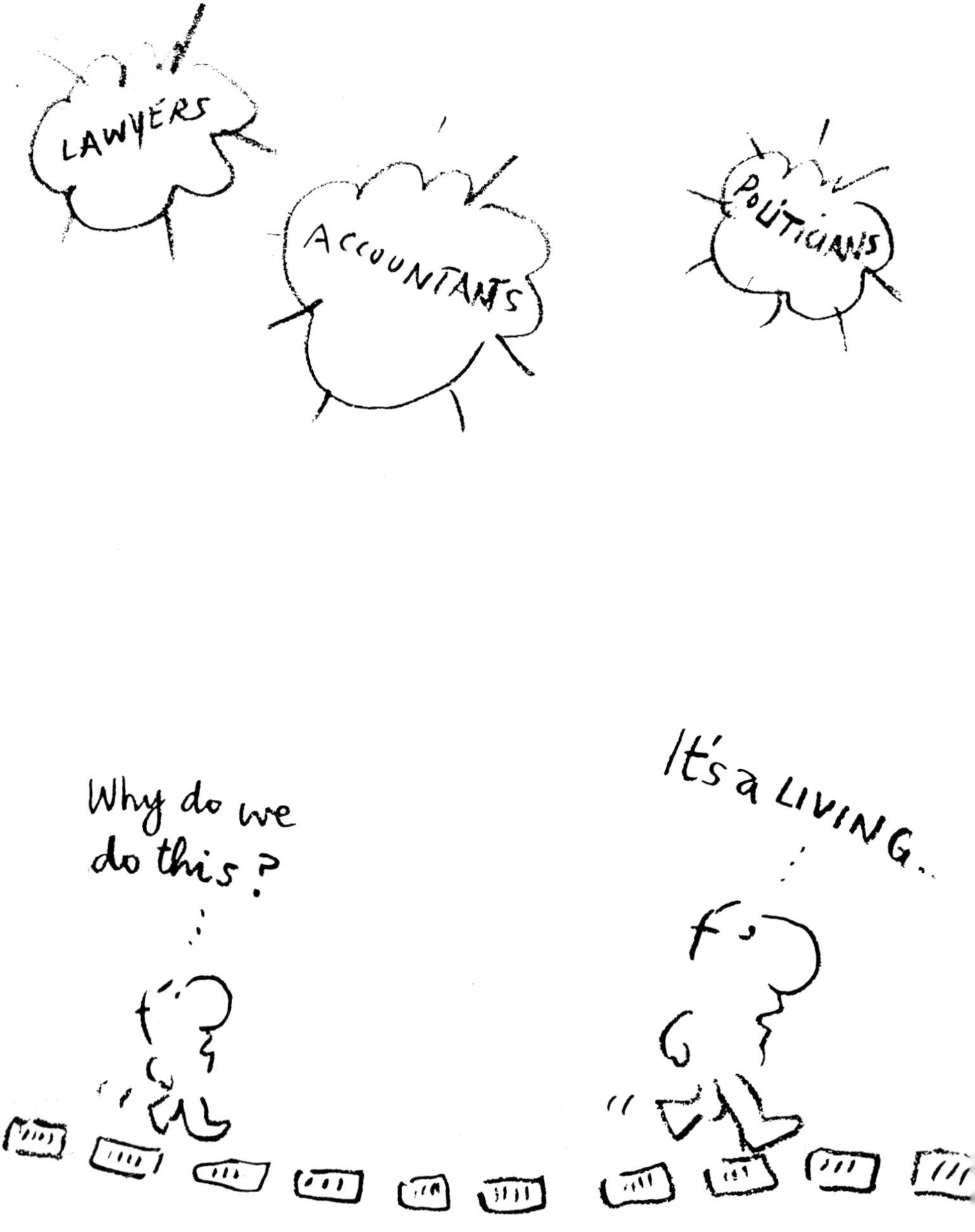
LAWYERS
ACCOUNTANTS
POLITICIANS
Why do we do this?
It's a LIVING..